M000047497

THE NINE
LIVES
OF CURIOUS
EDITH

Edith King Vosefski

THE NINE LIVES
OF CURIOUS EDITH

© Copyright 2020, Edith King Vosefski
All rights reserved.

All rights reserved. No portion of this book may be reproduced by
mechanical, photographic or electronic process, nor may it be stored
in a retrieval system, transmitted in any form or otherwise be copied
for public use or private use without written permission of the copyright owner.

Published by
Fig Factor Media, LLC | www.figfactormedia.com
Cover Design & Layout by Juan Pablo Ruiz

Printed in the United States of America

**FIG
FACTOR**
MEDIA

ISBN: 978-1-952779-13-8
Library of Congress Number: 2020923212

I dedicate this book to my favorite doctors who have made my life very enjoyable. They are Gerry and Jesse, Willy and Billy.

I am especially grateful to Gerry, who inspired the title of this book. He says I am like a cat with more than one life.

TABLE OF CONTENTS

Acknowledgements 6

Preface 7

Introduction 11

CHAPTER 1: A LIFE FROM LOVE 15

CHAPTER 2: THE YEARS OF GROWING RAPIDLY 23

CHAPTER 3: THE TEEN YEARS 33

CHAPTER 4: AN AMAZING YEAR.................................. 45

CHAPTER 5: PAJAMA GAMES...................................... 51

CHAPTER 6: A DINNER GUEST..................................... 61

CHAPTER 7: MUCH TO THINK ABOUT 69

CHAPTER 8: A LOOK TO THE FUTURE................................... 77

CHAPTER 9: MAKING QUICK PLANS 89

CHAPTER 10: A SACRED COVENANT....................................97

CHAPTER 11: DESTINATION MILWAUKEE 105

CHAPTER 12: FAMILY MATTERS 115

CHAPTER 13: ADVANCE TO SEATTLE 123

CHAPTER 14: FRIENDS AND VISITORS.................................131

CHAPTER 15: A NEW HORIZON 141

CHAPTER 16: LUCKY BREAKS 147

CHAPTER 17: THORNS AND ROSES........................157

CHAPTER 18: JOY, JOY AND MORE JOY............................ 167

CHAPTER 19: COURAGE AND TENACITY............................177

CHAPTER 20: CAN A SACRED GIFT BE A MIRACLE?.. 185

CHAPTER 21: SURPRISE, SURPRISE! 193

CHAPTER 22: ARTISTS IN RESIDENCE 203

CHAPTER 23: A VERY EXCITING TRIP....................................213

CHAPTER 24: LIVES IN TRANSITION 223

CHAPTER 25: ON THE JOB 233

CHAPTER 26: MY YEAR OFF 241

CHAPTER 27: OUT TO SEE THE WORLD............................ 249

CHAPTER 28: THE SEARCH FOR A NEW CAREER 257

CHAPTER 29: A DIFFERENT KIND OF TEACHING 267

CHAPTER 30: SURROUNDED BY GOLDEN LIGHT 279

CHAPTER 31: A LIFE WELL LIVED 291

Epilogue...300

ACKNOWLEDGEMENTS

There are many people who helped make it possible to have both the fun and the courage to write this book. I had a fall which broke my arm and almost detached it from my shoulder, but with the skill of an excellent orthopedic surgeon, he put everything back together with the use of a titanium rod. He turned me into a bionic woman, but it made handwriting difficult.

Soon after that, I had a stroke and was in the Marianjoy Rehabilitation Hospital. Thanks goes to all the wonderful doctors, therapists, and encouraging personnel there. Jennifer, my OT, convinced me that I could draw again and that it was possible to type an entire manuscript with the one finger that is functional. So I did that! It just takes grit.

Thanks also goes to the amazing publisher, Jackie Camacho-Ruiz; Nicholas Gatto, my chiropractor; and my friend, Rosa Castañeda, for all of their encouragement to write this book.

Special thanks to the wonderful people of St. Andrews who have prayed for me whenever I was on the prayer list. They include Mike Curtis, Sally Hedrick, Joanne Schupdach, and Mary Jane Haley.

Last but not least, a great big thanks to our Creator, who makes everything possible.

PREFACE

From the very first time I met Edith, I knew she was a dynamo of positive thinking and action. I was almost overpowered (but not completely) by her enthusiasm and her love of life and history. History was also my greatest interest and so immediately, we were on the same wavelength.

It was at that time, around 1976, that Edith picked up some "vibes" that I was not feeling in charge of my life. Not long afterwards, I received a book in the post from Edith that said "Are you happy with your life – if not, change it immediately! Not in a minute or two but now!" I did, and so I quickly learned not to enter a shop, restaurant, or hotel if I thought I did not want to pay their prices and NEVER to tell myself that I cannot afford to go in. I now happily go into interesting places, never looking at their price list. Sometimes it has been a shock but, in the end, it has all worked out well.

Edith was a truly great support to my sister and a talented decorative artist in her own right by encouraging Julia to develop her work and not allow it to be overshadowed by her husband's creativity.

Visits to historic houses were always a joy with Edith. Her curiosity for details and, I think a feeling that she would have lived a similar life to the great landowners of the past, matched my own romantic ideas.

Edith and Joe stayed with us for the last time during Christmas, 1986. She was at last able to visit the church where William Brewster had worshiped before leading the Puritan expedition to find a new settlement for their religious practices. We had arrived late, and the church was dark. For the first time I found Edith truly upset that she would not be able to go into the church. For once, I was masterful and managed to obtain the key and let us in. I even found the lights and Edith was transformed into her usual enthusiastic and appreciative self. She was also able to sign the register of all those direct descendants of Brewster and my reputation as a reliable guide was restored!

That same Christmas, Edith and Joe joined our family party. This was an occasion in which I excelled in vulgarity, providing a huge bottle of champagne and large, heavy, goblets. My Aunt Dorothy complained she couldn't lift them and my father said he didn't really like champagne! Edith and Joe obviously enjoyed the joke, because a year or so later we received a parcel with six huge wine glasses.

It's my pleasure to present Edith's memoir to the world. She certainly has been a positive influence on our family, and we have no doubt that as you read about her fascinating life, she will influence you as well. I hope you enjoy reading Edith's memoirs as much as I have.

—Andrew Brownfoot

www.andrewbrownfoot.com

Andrew is an artist, costume designer and author of several books including *High Fashion in Shakespeare's Time*, *High Fashion in Stuart Times*, and *Shakespeare on Stage*. He was a senior lecturer on all aspects of theatre design at the University of Central England, especially the history of fashion and style.

INTRODUCTION

If you were to ask me to describe myself in four words or less, I'd say thrifty, benevolent, curious, loving, and funny. Oops, that's five words, and they are all true.

The main focus of my adult life was my husband and the children we produced. I consider my marriage one of the great love stories of the twentieth century. Historically, so many of the classical love stories turn into tragedies, but unlike Romeo and Juliet, we managed to stay in love for sixty-two glorious years, until death sneaked in and separated us.

Most of my professional life falls into the field of education and I worked in many different kinds of schools: public, alternative, college, and in a psychiatric hospital as a teacher in an adolescent unit. I am a proud member of P.E.O. (Philanthropic Educational Organization) the women's group that sponsors scholarships for girls and women. It has grown into an international organization and has chapters all over the world. The organization may have helped to finance the PhD degrees for some of the up and coming women scientists.

There are many ways in which we as individuals make life better for others when we involve ourselves in groups that raise money or serve to advance the human race. The people to whom I have dedicated this book are all doctors of different specialties, and have helped me to enjoy my long life, and they are very dear to me. I have used their first names only, because if my memory isn't accurate, I wouldn't want to cause them any trouble.

I thank God for the many blessings and my exciting life, and I hope that you can find joy in the fact that the sun is going to rise tomorrow, and we can travel on together.

—Edith Vosefski

First Life

GROWING UP

Chapter 1

A LIFE FROM LOVE

———

I was born into a world where I sometimes felt out of time. In the wrong century, perhaps?

My personality seemed to be garrulous and taciturn at the same time. However, the garrulous side dominated. I learned to talk early and loved to tell jokes and stories. The day I was born, I only had four hairs on my head, but fortunately I grew a beautiful head of red hair, which I loved.

My parents were in their mid-forties and old enough to be my grandparents. However, they were hoping for a nice quiet infant, instead they received a dynamo. I was so filled with energy and curiosity that I wanted to explore the world. I loved the outdoors where I could observe worms, spiders, birds, squirrels, dogs and cats, but I ignored snakes. I played with the neighbor kids, especially the boys. We roller-skated, played catch, jumped rope, bicycled, and used a scooter, which wore the sole off my shoe. Yet when I had some quiet time, I read for hours, played dolls or paper dolls with girlfriends, and petted and loved my cat.

I was following a long line of distinguished ancestors and expected to grow up like a good little girl with manners of the Victorian era. That was 1930, when the Great Depression was in full sway. Life was very tough for many Americans as they lost their jobs, investments, and savings when the banks closed. Even some very wealthy people became destitute, seemingly overnight.

When my parents, Esther Livingston and Victor King, were married in 1926, they were reasonably well off. My father was a veteran of World War I. He was descended from two American Revolutionary soldiers and was very patriotic. He believed in American capitalism and invested in the stock market. By 1929, he had lost his entire portfolio and his job. He was a civil engineer, and very little building was taking place during the Great Depression. When I was born in 1930, my sweet parents told me that having a new baby was a joy and a real pick-me-up. Did I believe them? Of course.

My Mama was a little ball of energy, all of four-feet, eleven inches high. She liked to say she was five-feet tall with her shoes on. She wore her hair in a stylish bob and had deep blue eyes. She enjoyed talking with people. Her charming smile and gracious manners made her friends, neighbors, and family very comfortable in her presence.

My father was a handsome man with thick, silver hair and an inscrutable expression which manifested itself in being quiet. He was six-feet tall with his shoes on, so there was a big difference in my parent's heights. He loved to read history, but often entertained himself by working calculus or trigonometry problems, playing chess, or reading from all thirty volumes of the set of encyclopedias we had in our home. He was the product of a line of resolute New England Yankees and descended from William Brewster, the spiritual leader of the pilgrims who arrived on the Mayflower. This makes William Brewster my twelfth great grandfather. Our lineage in Europe goes back even further. Some genealogical research has revealed that I am the twenty-second great granddaughter of St. Margaret, Queen of Scotland, who converted her country to Christianity.

One of the memories I treasure was seeing my mother walk up to my father with a twinkle in her eyes, reach up, put a hand on his shoulder and ask "Vic, do you love me?" With a very solemn expression he replied, "Esther, I told you that once." They burst out laughing and with a kiss and a lasting hug, the little love scene was finished with smiles all around. It was a fine example of my father's dry sense of humor.

My sister, Elizabeth Mary King, was three years my elder. Like me, she also had red hair and delicate, light ivory skin. My Mama told me that when I was born, the doctor said to her, "Esther, you have another daughter, and she also has red hair." But Mama wasn't sure that was true because I only had four hairs and they were standing straight up. She decided the doctor probably was right since she was not wearing her glasses.

My sister, who called herself Lizzie, regarded me as a nuisance when I was able to walk and talk because she became a book worm at an early age. When she was reading, there was no way I could get her attention. However, we were united in our understanding of our father's sense of humor. When we didn't catch the joke, we would turn to Mama and ask, "Does Daddy really mean that?" She'd reply, "Watch his face; he often has a certain twinkle in his eyes when he's pulling our leg." Mama's jokes were sillier and child-focused, like "knock, knock, who's there?" We had a lot of fun with our parents, and their high moral standards, integrity, and love made us feel very secure. We were off to a really great start!

Our lives changed when our household increased to five people. My eighty-seven-year-old grandfather moved in with us. He had lived with my Dad's brother Pat for a short while. But Pat's fastidious wife was not happy with that arrangement. Thus, he made his home with us, and felt comfortable there.

Grandfather had lost his wife, Victoria Kehl King, in 1916 when she had a heart attack at the age of sixty-three. She was in her kitchen making donuts, and suddenly her heart stopped and in a split second she was on the floor. Her cat ran to her, sniffed and licked her face, then lay next to her and began an agonizing racket of meows, alerting the family to hurry into the kitchen. It was obvious that Victoria had already passed, and she was beyond earthly help.

So Grandfather Theodore had fourteen years as a lonesome widower and was happy to be part of the family again. However, our small, rental apartment was very crowded with one more person in the family. So we began the hunt for a suitable house at an affordable price, and luck was with us.

I was about a year-and-a-half old at the time of the move, so the memories of my very early childhood are a mixture of three actual memories which were enhanced with input from my mother. The actual move was to a big house in Joliet, two stories high, which belonged to a family named Foster. Mr. Foster was a licensed plumber and was able to work often, but at reduced prices. So he and his wife agreed to move into the basement of their house and make it comfortable. Then, they wanted to rent out the top two floors, with one family on the first floor and another on the second floor. The catch was the two families would need to share a kitchen, which was on the first floor.

Mr. Foster, knowing that this could make trouble, installed a table and a two-burner hot plate and two folding chairs in an alcove on the second floor. This made it possible for the upstairs family to have coffee and cereal. When the milk was delivered, the dairy would provide an insulated box with ice for the milk.

Downstairs, the King family lived with a living room, a sunroom, a formal dining room, two large bedrooms, and a very large, well-equipped kitchen. Lizzie shared a bedroom with me. My parents had the other bedroom, and Grandfather had a bed and a dresser in the sunroom. The house had three bathrooms: one on each floor and the third one in the basement.

I have a vivid memory of my grandfather from when I was two years old. My toy box was kept in the sunroom. Almost every morning, I would go in to see Grandpa, who sat in a Morris chair in front of a very large window with sun pouring in. The sunshine outlined his body, leaving an image of a dark silhouette, surrounded by a halo of the sun. Little me would occasionally walk over to him and crawl up onto his lap. He would put me down, grab his cane, and hold it straight out. After that, I grabbed the cane and we had a daily tug-of-war.

Another precious memory from that period of my life was at Christmas when I was two or three years old. Our landlady, Mrs. Foster, wore gold earrings and they fascinated me. When anyone would ask me what I'd like Santa to bring me I replied, "Earrings!" In those days, you could buy plastic earrings at the Woolworth's dime store. They were fastened to a cardboard rectangle with two holes and the back of the earring was curved and slipped into the holes.

On Christmas morning, when I opened my first gift, I wasn't sure what I was looking at because all I saw were small cardboard pieces, three or four inches square, with round plastic dots in them. I didn't recognize them as earrings since I had only seen earrings on Mrs. Foster's ears, not in a package. Someone explained to me what they were and how they could clip onto my little ears. They did! Mama brought a hand mirror so I could see myself, and I was delighted.

Then, the fun began. My dad and Mr. Foster, who I called Uncle Charlie, took the pile of earring cards, sat down on the floor and started stacking the cards, one on top of the other. Uncle Charlie did the stacking and my dad put his hands on the outer edges of the cards to steady them.... so they kept stacking. Then they asked me to stand next to the pile because they wanted to find out if I was as tall as their stack. They had a hard time holding it together, and it collapsed so we never found out if the stack was as tall as me. Within the next six months, most of the earrings disappeared and I never wore earrings again until I was in college.

The third memory is still on my mind. I remember how my love of folk music and lore began when I was two or three. The Fosters grew up in the back hills of Appalachia and were surrounded by Irish, Scots, and English who had immigrated a century earlier. They had grown up steeped in the songs and stories of their neighbor's ancestors.

Mable Foster would take my sister Lizzy and me out to the big front porch and sit me on her lap with Lizzie usually sitting on the floor near us. Then the music began. She would sing for what was probably an hour. If one of the songs was really funny, she would repeat it and we learned to sing it with her. I have never forgotten the song, "*Old Dan Tucker*" and how he "*combed his hair with a wagon wheel.*" Some days, the radio would feature Burl Ives, and we would sit and sing with him.

Now, in my old age as I'm writing this, I have a very large collection of international folk songs. I often sing along with the tapes and discs. At the moment, I am working on Native American chants and songs. I enjoy learning something new. An old dog can learn new tricks if she is determined.

Chapter 2

THE YEARS OF GROWING RAPIDLY

In 1933, my father was offered a job as the superintendent of a CCC Camp. The program helped unemployed, unmarried men between the ages of 18 and 25. The program was known by the three letters which stood for the Civilian Conservation Corps.

My Dad had been in the Army Corps of Engineers during WW I, and the camps were run like the military. The young men received a monthly stipend but were required to send most of the money they earned to their family, since they received room, board, and clothing. This was considered the most successful program offered during the Great Depression by FDR's administration.

Dad was pleased to be working again, and we left Joliet and moved to Downers Grove, Illinois, a town about twenty miles outside of Chicago, where Mama started her teaching career. It was a charming small town with paved streets, Mama and pop grocery stores, and a dairy which delivered milk to your door. If you needed ice, a horse-drawn truck delivered it to your indoor ice box. You could order either twenty or fifty pounds of ice by putting a large card in your front window, which showed the amount you wanted. My first paid job was putting the sign in our window.

Both my parents believed and taught us that everyone in a family should share the work. They paid us very small amounts of money when we did chores in order to teach us how to budget, save, donate, and develop a work ethic. Hence, my job was to check the icebox daily before breakfast and pull out the drip pan that collected the melted water. The ice box was four steps lower than the kitchen, in an alcove next to the back door. In warm weather, I would throw the water out into the yard. In winter, I used towels to soak up the water and dried the pan. I was paid forty cents a week. I was so happy to have enough to go to the Prince Castle Ice Cream Store and buy a double dip cone for ten cents and put thirty cents in the piggy bank. Pretty neat for a kid who was not quite four years old!

I considered being able to get ice cream without having to ask for money, such an incredible thing that I decided to apply for another job. For as long as I can remember, I have always liked things that sparkle or are shiny and unwrinkled. So I volunteered to polish everyone's shoes every Saturday night. Then we would have clean, shiny shoes to wear to church in the morning. My pay was fifty cents. I donated twenty-five cents to the Sunday school collection, and the other quarter would pay for a movie at the Tivoli Theater in town. It cost ten cents for admission, ten cents for a box of popcorn, and a nickel for some candy. A lovely bargain.

Every Saturday afternoon, the Tivoli Theater would show weekly serials such as *Roy Rogers, The Perils of Pauline, The Lone Ranger, etc.* Our little town was proud of our theater, as it was the second one in the country to show talking pictures. It still exists today and is owned by a local family.

I was happy to be able to see movies and went as often as I could. The films had characters who were brave, honest, and courageous. I watched them from the edge of my seat, holding my breath. It was veryexciting.

Of course, there was more to life than petty jobs and movies. I attended kindergarten and first grade at Whitier School, and it was about to create a new me. Until I started school, I was a real tomboy. I climbed trees, I raced around the block on my second hand bicycle, ran races with the neighborhood boys, and liked being outdoors. I loved kindergarten. I made new friends, and we played games, sang songs, and had fun.

First grade was much more serious. I learned to read. My first book was stupid, but I can still repeat the words. However, that book worked and soon, I became a skilled reader. That simple story has been stuck in my head for eighty-four years and I don't know why. Perhaps it's because it gave me a wonderful gift-- the ability to read--which has become a lifelong passion. Would you believe that a simple story about three rabbits hopping into the woods could be the fundamental step to appreciating classical literature?

Being a schoolgirl required a wardrobe. I often wore my sister's hand-me-downs. I considered it a normal way to acquire clothes. Lizzie was a child with good taste, and I looked forward to being able to fit into some of her clothes, which I thought were very pretty.

In first grade, I had a classmate named Marilyn, who was a Shirley Temple wannabe with lots of blond curls and expensive clothes, similar to those of the famous child star. She strutted up to me with a superior sneer on her face, stood in front of me, looked me over and said in a very taunting voice, "You've got your sister's dress on." I turned to Marilyn and said, "So what's it to you if I do?" and I walked away. I didn't care what she thought. But somehow, the incident spread like wildfire. Local gossip reported that Marilyn got her expensive clothes from an uncle with mob connections. True? I have no idea.

In second grade, if you did something bad, you had to stand in the corner. One day, the corner was full and when I got caught talking to a classmate, the teacher put me out in the hallway. Then she forgot about me. It was very boring, so to entertain myself, I put my arms out on either side of me. Then I started turning myself around, facing the wall, then facing the hall. Facing the wall, then facing the hall, with my arms out, traveling down the hallway. Suddenly, I felt my hand hit something. I had knocked the fire extinguisher off the wall and onto the floor. It landed on its head and began spewing the white foam all over the hallway. I was terrified so I ran into the washroom and hid in a stall. But then I heard the bell ring for recess and all the girls ran into the washroom as they always did before they went outside. They were all excited and talking about the fire extinguisher. Nobody could figure out what happened, but I wasn't going to tell them. I ran outside with everyone else, and I never did anything like that again or told anybody about it. Till now.

Second grade passed by quickly, and third grade introduced something new. Geography was part of the curriculum, and the textbook was entitled, *If I Were Going*. It covered many European countries and told about the people and what they wore. It was also written more like a folk tale. This made geography very interesting and I learned to read maps. I loved maps and could entertain myself with them for a long time. I decided that someday I would travel and see the world. So far, I have visited twenty-seven countries in a period of twenty-five years. More about this later.

When I finished fifth grade, my six years at Whitier School came to an end because it was only a K-5 school. To complete the rest of the grades, we had to attend Washington School, which was a new adventure.

In May, my family bought our first house, and we moved to 4832 Bryan Place, on the north side of town just a couple blocks from the train tracks and the Tivoli Theater. My new school was only a block away, so I could come home for lunch. Little did I suspect that this would be my home for the next seventy-five years.

* * * * *

The fall of 1941 was a time of high tension and worry when school started that September. The Nazis of Germany had invaded Poland and were busy trying to conquer much of Europe and Britain. Shortly before Thanksgiving, the government of the United States and its citizens were anticipating the possibility of entering the war. On December 7, 1941, the Japanese attacked our naval station in Pearl Harbor, Hawaii.

I can still remember that day. It was Sunday afternoon, and I was eleven years old. Classical music was playing on the radio by a symphony orchestra. I was alone, sitting peacefully enjoying the music when it stopped and an announcer said, "WE INTERRUPT THIS PROGRAM TO TELL YOU THAT THE NAVAL STATION AT PEARL HARBOR HAS BEEN ATTACKED BY THE JAPANESE." My heart jumped up, frightening me, and I wondered if we would be safe living in the Midwest. I rushed into the family room where my father was napping on the daybed. I woke him with the news. He grabbed my hand as if to reassure me and we walked together to where the radio was playing and listened to the horrible details of the attack. By the next day, President Roosevelt had announced that Congress had declared war on the Japanese and we had entered World War ll.

The schools helped to raise money for the war by having bond booklets available. Any kid who wanted to contribute would bring money to buy a stamp worth ten cents. The stamps were placed in the booklet, and when the booklet was full, it was worth eighteen dollars. When the bond matured a few years later, it was worth twenty-five dollars. You took the full booklet to the local post office to cash it and receive the money.

The next big adjustment for American citizens was rationing. Everyone was only allowed to purchase a limited amount of meat, butter, sugar, and flour. We had three meatless meals a week. On the meatless days, we ate canned fish, eggs, or cereal for supper.

We had a neighbor who had a son in the Marines. He was able to secure a seven-day leave to come home to be married. One day, his mother knocked on our door, and asked us if we could spare a half cup of butter and three-fourths of a cup of flour to take to the local bakery to make the wedding cake. The bakery was also strictly rationed and allotted specific amounts of ingredients for the various foods they made. Both the future mother-in-law and the groom's mother collected the small amounts required for a very large cake.

Sometime that winter, I became ill and developed anemia. Our doctor petitioned the Ration Board to give my family extra stamps so the butcher could give us more liver to correct my red cell deficiency. It worked, but I hated it. I gave up eating liver for the rest of my life.

Years later, whenever I cooked liver for my family, our little half beagle sneaked under the dining room table and whimpered as if he were going to die if we didn't share the liver. I then left the table, went into the kitchen and gave my portion to Blacky. He was a very happy dog.

Sixth grade was coming to an end, and that was the year that many of the girls began to think that boys were no longer poison. We had our secret little crushes. Adolescence was on the horizon.

The war also changed my father's employment. The CCC program came to an end. The young men either volunteered to join the armed services, or they were drafted. Dad was a civil engineer with years of experience managing construction crews. The CCC men constructed buildings, roads, bridges, and land management projects, like the state parks. Dad's experience as a veteran of WW1, combined with his management skills at the camp, got him hired by a big steel company located in northern Indiana, a short distance from Chicago.

This created a family problem. The round trip from Downers to Whiting, Indiana was about sixty miles. Even though this job was classified as essential to the war effort, gasoline was so strictly rationed he couldn't drive to the job every day. Luckily, his sister Grace lived in Hyde Park in

Chicago and she had an extra bed. He could stay there and have enough gas to get to work every day. He came home on Wednesday evening and spent the night with us. He was usually home for the weekend too, so it worked out quite well.

Chapter 3

THE TEEN YEARS

I met my dearest friend, Arden Stephens, when we were in seventh grade. We became so close that we were like two peas in a pod. We had so many interests in common that we would be called soulmates in the current system of labeling people. I realize the term seems to suggest you only have one soulmate. For some that may be true, but I am sure such a definition is too limiting. If you are a loving person, you can love several people so deeply that they have a permanent place in your heart. Arden and I kept our friendship going for more than seventy years, and you will meet her throughout this book.

In 1944, we graduated from eighth grade and entered high school after a summer of exciting opportunities. Downers Grove had a new park district, and they sponsored a wartime pageant. Mildred Zook Dickinson was an outstanding modern dance teacher, who was a student of Martha Graham, and had been married to the famous architect, Harold Zook. Mildred did the choreography for the pageant. Since Arden and I were in her weekly dance class, we were in the show. We danced to the *Warsaw Concerto.*

Neither Arden nor I dated much in high school. The summer after our sophomore year, we both had the opportunity to attend summer camp. Prior to leaving, Arden said, "Maybe I can meet some nice boy who will like me. After all, we're almost sixteen and have never been kissed." That wasn't a problem I worried about. I was too wrapped up in dancing.

Arden went to a camp situated on the shore of Lake Michigan, in Saugatuck, Michigan. I was off to Steamboat Springs, Colorado to attend the Perry Mansfield Camp, elevation seven thousand feet.

The camp had girls who were seven through ten years old, on up to adults. Many of them were from very wealthy families and were there to perfect their horseback riding. Some of the girls also had bodyguards on the grounds because their millionaire parents were getting a divorce and were all over the news. It was not exactly a typical environment for me.

I was also able to take a riding class. But my chief reason for being there was they had an outstanding theater program, and a great dance program too. We exercised about four hours every day and had rehearsals for another four hours after supper. We were in tip top shape in about three weeks. One day, one of the girls came to tell me to go to the office because there was a telegram for me. I couldn't imagine who might send me a telegram. I opened it and it read, "On the beach with Richard Allbers!! Signed, Sweet Sixteen." Needless to say, it came from Arden.

By the end of the seven weeks I was seriously thinking that I might like to become a dance major in college. The curriculum was full of anatomy and physiology. It prepared you for a physical education teaching certificate, because the most likely employment for a dance major was as a gym teacher, who could teach dance. Either that, or you could open your own dance studio.

You have probably already figured out that the camp, and getting there, was very expensive. My first summer I was on a work scholarship. That meant that I would serve as a kitchen helper from six-thirty until eight thirty in the morning as a server at breakfast.

After my first morning shift, I would have a voice lesson. At nine o' clock, I had a half hour class called Body Mechanics, which was a fancy name for a head-to-toe exercise class. At nine-thirty, I had an hour class of horseback riding. I really enjoyed meeting the horses and learning how sensitive and smart they seem to be. I got fairly good at trotting, but never mastered cantering well.

At eleven o'clock, modern dance started with stretching exercises and creativity in movements. At noon, I served again as a waitress.

Since we were in the midst of the Rockies, everything was located either up or down, so the first weeks' worth of sore muscles made walking a bit challenging. In the afternoon, there were more classes, and I had one more job to do.

Lowell Whitman, a gentleman who had spent his life in the area, was in charge of a boy's camp about a mile from Perry-Mansfield. Every summer he would have a typical western style bar-b-que and invite the whole town of Steamboat Springs, including our camp. On the first day of camp in the morning, a local rodeo was held in Steamboat, presented by local cowboys who demonstrated calf roping, riding bucking horses, and other and various skills which were part of their real job. It was very exciting. One of the requirements of living at that altitude was to have a cowboy style hat. If you've ever seen a western type movie and wondered why every guy in it was always wearing a hat, here's the answer: bare heads can lead to sunstroke at higher altitudes. The girls who made up the horsey set would buy their western hat and immediately throw it on the ground when they returned to camp. They'd stamp on it, rub it into the dirt, and shake it and reshape it, so they didn't look like greenhorns.

We all wore our hats to the bar-b-que, because the pit was in the open and it was bright and sunny that day. Two or three days before the guests arrived, the host dug a pit six to eight feet long, and wide enough to hold a metal grill with a side of beef, and some other kind of meat. The pit was deep and the bottom was lined with rocks. Under the rocks they lined the pit with natural materials to create a very hot fire which made the large rocks so warm that they stayed hot for two days. While the ranch hands were attending to the meat, the guests received their plates and proceeded to the tables covered with food. They filled their plates, then went to the pit to get their meat. It was a magnificent feast and I was so impressed that someone would invite a whole town to their bar-b-que.

* * * * *

In February of the next year, my father got a new construction job in Paris, Illinois. And once again, the distance was far enough away that he had to get a room there. He came home on Friday evening and left again on Sunday evening. One Sunday in February of 1947, as it was still getting dark, he left early and picked up another engineer, who worked on the same project. Driving on Route 1, the highway was higher than the surrounding land on either side of the highway. Dad was driving at the speed limit which was 50 mph, and the road was free of ice or snow. All of a sudden, as Dad's car passed a gravel country road, a car driven by a drunk driver came flying through the intersection, broadsiding Dad's car. My dad's passenger flew through the windshield and died instantly. The car careened off the road and tumbled down the embankment, turning over twice until it landed in a pasture below the road. The cars at that time had no seat belts, cell phones, or onboard system to alert someone of the accident. Dad landed in the pasture. I'm not sure if the drunk stayed around, but another man came upon the scene and drove to the nearest farm. He asked the farmer to call the police and send an ambulance. My father and the dead passenger were escorted to the little hospital in Watseca, Illinois. Using my father's driver's license, the police got in touch with the Downers Grove police department and asked if someone would go to our home to tell the family what had happened.

When the squad car drove up to our house, Mrs. Rokar, a neighbor living across the street from us and our next door neighbor Mrs. Cowart, ran over to my mother's, bless their hearts, so my mother was not alone when she got the news.

Mama called my Uncle Pat, Dad's brother who lived in South Bend, Indiana, two and a half hours from Watseca. She told him that we would meet him at the hospital as soon as we could get there. In the meantime, one of the neighbors called yet another friend of Mama's, who volunteered to drive her to Watseca.

By the time Lizzie and I got home from school, my mother was gone. The neighbors told us what happened and we were devastated. Even though my dad was away a lot, my dad and I were close. When he was home, though, he gave us so much attention and love. How could this be happening?

The next day mother called us.

"The doctors don't have much hope for your father," she

said. "I think you and Lizzie should come to Watseca." We were devastated and made arrangements to take the train to Chicago and begin our journey to Watseca the next day. We didn't get there until ten o'clock in the evening.

Dad was semi-conscious for two days. Then, he died from internal bleeding from punctured lungs and more. Luckily, my mother was there to hear some of his last words and be with him when he passed.

After all the funeral arrangements were made, we went to the funeral home. That was the first time I had ever seen a dead person or been to a funeral. I was sixteen years old. My father was in an open casket. His head had not been smashed, but the person who groomed him for the casket had parted his hair on the wrong side. That little detail bothered me so much that I whipped a comb out of my purse and changed it, while bursting into tears. It's amazing how alive that memory is. I can still see it.

When I went back to school, I was surrounded by friends and acquaintances who did their best to comfort me. I struggled with my faith for quite a while and became agnostic. It seemed that camp was the only thing I had to look forward to again.

* * * * *

I was fortunate enough to attend camp the next summer too but earned my way by chaperoning another girl from the area who was also going to Perry Mansfield Summer Camp. Her mother had purchased tickets on the Denver Zephyr from Chicago Union Station. It was a luxury train that had a second story with observation windows to view the scenery. I occupied a seat in a car for people who would sleep at night sitting in their seat for the entire trip, but fortunately the seat reclined a little. Most of the day, I went up to the observation deck and watched as we crossed the Mississippi River, and the States of Iowa, Kansas, and Nebraska. We enjoyed trips to the dining car. The food was delicious, and I shared a table with three other people, so the conversation was stimulating.

By early morning as the sun streamed into our windows and woke most of us, there were moans and groans as people stood up to discover sitting up all night was not the ideal way to sleep. We rushed to the bathrooms and I did my best to try to look presentable.

The train arrived in Denver about eight o'clock in the morning. Lugging our heavy suitcases, we entered a bus that was waiting for campers who dismounted from the Zephyr. The driver had a list of all the passengers who were expected and called roll. When everyone was accounted for, the bus carried us to another station that served the Denver, Salt Lake, and Rio Grande Railway.

Before the bus driver would open the door, he gave us some idea of what we were going to experience on the next leg of the trip, which would take almost seven hours. This was 1946, and the engine on our train was an old fashioned, coal-fired steam engine. The driver explained that we would go over the continental divide and reach an altitude of fourteen thousand feet. He also explained that we would pass through the Moffat Tunnel, the world's longest railroad tunnel. It was six miles long, and there would be nothing to see as we passed through it.

However, we were not prepared for the experience we suffered. As we entered the tunnel, the train lost much of the light inside it. As a tunnel is a hole with a cover over it, so the smoke from the engine was forced to drift back over the cars and fill them with smoke. By the time we were halfway through the tunnel, there was so much smoke, the other end of the car was invisible. Coughing and sneezing began, our faces and hands were turning black, and breathing became more difficult. I became comrades with the other girls taking the trip to get to camp and we told jokes and had a few creative comments. It was an amazing experience.

When we reached fourteen thousand feet my nose began to bleed. But I was not alone. It happened to several people, and I think it must be a common experience because the conductor came into the car carrying paper towels and Kleenex tissues. We must have been a frightful sight when we arrived at camp, with bloody noses and smoked faces. The only water on the train came with the box lunches we were served, but in spite of it all, we rallied together, and I definitely considered it a wild experience and a real adventure.

During my second summer at camp, I was assigned to work in the vegetable garden. I remember my friend Portia and I would eat so many of the raw peas as we were collecting them, that someone once passed by and said, "Are you going to leave any for dinner?" It was interesting because it was irrigated, and I had to open or close the little sluice gates at times. Often, I had another girl join me and we would either weed or pick when the plants were ripe.

The summer passed quickly and after the seven fun, but physically grueling weeks, I was eager to return home and wait for Mrs. Dickinson to start her dance class again. This was my junior year, and there was much to learn. I tried out for a part in the fall junior play, *Little Women*, and I got to play Mrs. March, the mother. Arden was on the makeup crew and painted wrinkles on my face so I would look older. Now that I have real wrinkles, I wish I could just wipe them off like I did that day.

One night on stage, we heard a knock on the set door, but when we opened it, the actor wasn't there. He missed his cue because he was just fooling around backstage. Someone had to say something to keep the show going, so I said, "Oh if he's not at the door anymore, he must be having trouble tying up his horse. Maybe we should go see if he needs help." One of the boys on stage with me went with the suggestion and left the set. He managed to find the actor backstage and bring him into the scene while we continued ad libbing to keep the audience entertained. I don't know if the audience caught on, or not. I hope not.

Second Life

YOUNG ADULTHOOD

Chapter 4

AN AMAZING YEAR

———

The year was 1952 and it was my senior year at Northwestern. During the previous year, I had struggled with my religious beliefs and I went to Canterbury House, the Episcopal student center on campus, for instructions and counseling. There I met Father Maxwell, a young, Episcopal priest who was very good at his job. In May of my junior year, I was confirmed in the Episcopal church which made me an Anglican Catholic. I have spent the rest of my long life doing my best to live up to the commandments, honoring Jesus, and respecting all human beings regardless of race or color. I am sharing this with you because my faith has had a profound effect on my life. Now, I'm going to lighten up so you can share my amazement.

I knew that I no longer wanted to pursue my theatrical education. I added a teaching course to qualify me to teach public speaking or theatrical courses at the high school level. This was a pragmatic decision that could lead to a solid career. I felt that teaching was in my blood. My mother and two of her sisters were teachers and one of my father's sisters was a teacher too. Looking back on my Livingston ancestors, there was a long line of headmasters in Ulster.

As fate would have it, I was offered a job in an institution which belonged to the Episcopal Diocese of Chicago. Eager to find out what the position actually required, I made an appointment for an interview in April at Lawrence Hall, a home for boys located on the north side of Chicago. They needed me in the summer, but I was not available until classes ended in June. I told them if they could wait, I could start on June first after I graduated.

Unknown to me, the minute I stepped through the door of Lawrence Hall, my life would change forever! The building was large enough to house one hundred boys and staff. The boys ranged in age from six to seventeen and stayed in dormitories that held about twenty kids each. The boys were grouped by age, in two-year increments like five and six-year-olds, seven and eight-year-olds, etc. The staff had private bedrooms. I was impressed.

Father Curzon was in charge. He was a graying man in his fifties who seemed very friendly. He explained that most of the boys were victims of broken homes. Some were orphans or had a father who left the family and the single mother had no one to help her and was having trouble raising her son. Some of the boys were placed there temporarily until a situation with their parents was resolved so they would not be used as pawns in the conflict. Wow! This was a serious job.

After I learned the big picture of what to expect, I was still listening. I decided to take a tour of the building, which included introductions to staff members. My tour guide was Dewey, a blond, middle-aged man who was in charge of all the maintenance at the building. I saw the dorms, the Chapel, the offices, a dining room which could hold one hundred-fifty people, and the kitchen.

When we entered the kitchen, the dietitian was busy conferring with a tall, skinny young man. So Dewey opened the refrigerator alcove where the food was stored which also had a large freezer area. It was the size of a small room and had stacks and stacks of egg cartons. We returned to the kitchen. The dietitian did not live on campus and was preparing to leave for the day. Dewey quickly introduced me to her, and as she went out the door, the skinny young man, who was about two years older than me, rushed over to introduce himself.

"Hi my name is Joe, what's your name?"

He startled me. Why was he introducing himself, I wondered?

"I'm Edith," I replied.

"Are you going to be working here?" he asked.

"Probably, not settled yet."

"I hope you will. I'll cross my fingers for you."

I thought that was kind of cute but couldn't figure out why he would care so much about whether I got the job or not. But I knew I had to go.

"Thanks. I see that Dewey wants us to move on," I said to him, walking away. "Bye."

The tour was over, and I was escorted to the office of Father Curzon. Sitting in the office was his wife, and he introduced us. She started chatting with me and asking a lot of questions. We had a very pleasant conversation and she was definitely charming. However, I was sure she was there to give her husband a second opinion on me. I must have passed inspection because I was offered the position.

I arrived at Lawrence Hall on June first, as scheduled, with suitcase in hand and very eager to get started. I was told that the boys go to camp all July and the first two weeks of August, so they wanted me to act as housemother to the six and seven-year-olds in their dorm until they left for camp. How's that for a surprise? I wouldn't be twenty-two years old until August, and I was going to be the mother figure for twenty-three kids! Wow! I also was asked to be a speech coach for all the boys at Lawrence Hall. They also said that I wouldn't need to stay for the summer when the boys were gone. However, they offered this option.

"You are welcome to stay here if you would like to remain in the city, and this could give you the chance to work on the speech program you are creating for us," said Father Curzon. "Most of the staff will be here because this is the time when much of the maintenance work is done. The dietitian and Joe will be working on planning several months of menus and figuring out the dates to place the orders so food will be available."

I left the office a bit bewildered, thinking about whether or not I'd be staying for the summer and what that would entail. Just then, Joe came along, picked up my suitcase and escorted me to my room. He seemed to be such a helpful, polite guy.

"Do you need any help with anything?" he asked.

"No thank you. One of the housemothers of the older boys is going to coach me about an hour from now, so I'm going to unpack my suitcase and hang up my clothes. Is there a place to iron around here?"

"Yeah, across the hall, three doors to the left."

I picked up my suitcase, put it on the bed, and started unpacking, without looking at him further. Joe took the hint and departed.

Betty, the housemother, came to visit shortly thereafter. She was in charge of the older, ten to twelve-year boys and was probably in her thirties. I told her I was rather nervous because I had no brothers and no direct experience in knowing how boys might act. She put my mind at ease immediately.

"Edith, relax," Betty replied. "You are going to be okay. I know you aren't going to let a bunch of six-year-olds run your dorm, right? If any of us hears a commotion coming from the dorm, someone will be there quickly to help you. So don't give it another thought. Needing help won't be held against you. You are going to do fine. Now, I should get back to my dorm because the kids are about to arrive home on the school bus. Check with you later." With that, she left me to my fate.

From the first day I met my group of five and six-year olds, I enjoyed getting to know them and making them laugh. As for the staff, I soon became part of a team that was a true pleasure to work with. Everyone at Lawrence Hall really had a mission to serve the boys with love and help them find their way in life. There was a camaraderie among the team, and everyone treated each other with respect, and as an equal. Nobody's job was more important than anyone else's.

Everyone was Christian and was truly living out their values, including the "golden rule" of treating others like they would like to be treated. We all tried to live by the Ten Commandments and the way Jesus wanted us to live. It was a loving, forgiving atmosphere for boys who at times, could be downright challenging and unlovable, as the result of their life experiences.

I have to admit that keeping twenty-three little boys in line was a challenge, especially at first. At times, I had to think and react quickly. But they responded to my humor and playful nature, because I liked to have fun and create fun for them too. I learned what worked for them and what didn't and after a while, it all came naturally. I felt I was in the right place at the right time, and Lawrence Hall began to feel like home.

Chapter 5

Pajama Games

———

My little charges always kept me on my toes. During my first week, I settled into their bedtime routine of having the boys wash up, get into their pajamas and be in their bunks by eight o' clock. Then there was a quiet time, until lights out at eight-thirty. For three nights I read them a story, and then we turned out the lights, with the exception of the glowing nightlights which led the way to the bathroom.

The sixth day of the week was laundry day, or to say it more accurately, Friday night was laundry night. Our dorm's laundry room was attached at the far end of the dorm adjacent to the bathroom. There was no door on it, so if I was in there, I could almost see and could certainly hear what was happening with the kids. The room was furnished with hampers, a large folding table, and carts to take the laundry out for pick up by a commercial laundry around seven o' clock the next morning. All of the clothes had to be folded, pockets emptied, and zippers closed. Multiply this by twenty-three for every item of clothing worn in a week and you can see that it could take all night. I figured I'd find another time to do the bulk of it, so Friday night would consist only of the clothes the kids had worn on Friday.

I went into the laundry room during quiet time, since it seemed like I had the most success getting the laundry done at that time. I was double-checking I had all the clothes I needed and intended to be back in the dorm in a minute or two, expecting they would all be quiet or safely asleep. But on this particular Friday night, just as I picked up the first garment, all hell broke loose. There was laughter, clapping, and words flying through the air. When I stepped back into the dorm, I didn't know whether I wanted to laugh or cry. Three boys were standing up on the top bunk having a peeing contest. They were trying to see who could hit the guy across the aisle. I took a deep breath and was just about to yell at them to stop when Joe came rushing in and took over. Nice, quiet Joe instantly turned into top Sergeant Joe, and he ordered the boys to get off the top bunks.

"You guys are being very disrespectful to Miss Edith," he barked, "and that's not a good thing. Right now you owe her an apology. I said NOW. Let's hear it!!" His last statement was almost a shout. But giving an apology was an entirely new idea to the boys, or else they didn't understand the word. Either way, they just stared at us blankly. At least they were subdued for now.

"I don't want to hear another sound from you while I speak with Edith," Joe finished as he turned to me.

Joe looked me straight in the eye and lowered his voice.

"Edith, I'll handle seeing to whatever needs to be done. I will strip the beds, get the clean sheets, and make the beds. I'll stay until everyone is asleep," he said. "You go get the laundry started or you'll be up all night." I immediately felt relieved and happy to have the help. I began to think Joe was wonderful. I left to do the laundry.

Close to an hour later, Joe entered the laundry room and without a word, started helping me finish zipping all the jeans. Of course, I thanked him for his rescue and praised his help and service. He shook his head in acknowledgment and smiled. Perhaps two minutes later, he leaned across the table, kissed me on the cheek and said, "You are going to marry me."

I was taken aback. "You're crazy," I replied. "I don't even know you, and you don't really know me either."

"Well, when you really get to know me, you'll change your mind," he replied impishly. "Looks like we're finished. It must be ninety-eight degrees in here. Why don't I take the cart down and you can wash the sweat off your face and meet me downstairs? Let's have a cold drink together."

That was just what we needed. I was exhausted but met Joe downstairs anyway. He had gotten us some glasses of ginger ale with plenty of ice to cool us off. I had a lot to think about. I just had received my first kiss from a man (even though it was on the cheek) who told me he wanted to marry me before our first date. We chatted into the night, and it was the start of a great friendship.

June was passing quickly. The Chicago schools had closed, so the kids were with us all day. They played various games and a group of staff members would take them to a nearby park where they had swings, monkey bars, slides, etc. to have some fun and use up a bit of their energy. Older boys played baseball or ran around a rough track.

I resurrected singing games from my childhood, and the youngest learned to sing the *Farmer In the Dell, and London Bridge Is Falling Down.* I changed the last words of *"London Bridge"* to "my fair Brady," to let the fair lady have the day off. In the dorm next to us there were eight and nine-year-old boys, and the next thing I knew, they came over to me with their housemother and asked to play with us. Our games were very physical, and they enjoyed falling down, capturing another person, and sending him off to jail.

After the games, the children and I returned to the dorm to sort out the clothes that the boys would need for camp. It was a major job and also involved shopping for some of them. They needed sturdy jeans, t-shirts, and bathing suits. I did not take any of the boys with me to the stores, but they found their way there anyway.

One June summer day, two of our boys, Johnny and David wandered off the property. It was easy to do because we had no fence or gates. However, the neighborhood police knew about the boys at the Hall and when they saw them walking around aimlessly, they picked them up. The only thing the boys had done wrong was leave without permission. But I guess their taste of freedom made them want to try it again.

A few days later, Johnny and David went out to play and disappeared again! Amazingly, nobody knew they were gone. Once again, the police brought them home in a squad car. At dinnertime, they were right in their spot and when we returned to the dorm to get ready for bed, I saw them take out brand new pajamas, complete with price tags attached. I took a few seconds to reflect on the situation. Then I asked Johnny to come and sit with me on a nearby bench.

"Johnny, where did you get those pajamas?" I asked kindly.

"Aren't they nice? Very soft," replied Johnny.

"I asked you where you got them."

"At the store."

"How did you pay for them?"

"What do you mean; what's pay mean?"

"When we go into a store, we have to give money for what we buy," I explained.   "

"But I don't have any money," he protested rather loudly.

"That's why you can't ever do this again unless you have money," I replied. "What you did is called shoplifting, and it is against the law. The police can arrest you," I told him in a very serious voice. "It is a very bad thing to do."

"But, David did it too; we did it together! Will we go to jail?" I looked up to see David standing before us and said, "David, have you been listening to what Johnny and I have been talking about?" David shook his head yes.

"Come and sit with us."

By now the other boys had become interested in our conversation. They began surrounding David and walking over to us too. I noticed it immediately.

"The rest of you boys can back off. We do not need to be surrounded," I said, halting their advances and sending them walking away from us in different directions. David hesitantly joined us on the bench.

"Tell me what you have learned by listening," I said.

David looked worried. He was wringing his hands and close to tears.

"Stealing is very bad, and no one should do it," he said quietly. "In Sunday school, I learned that word. I heard that God has a law against it, but I didn't know what we did was what they were talking about." Then he burst into tears.

I put my arm around both boys for a hug. Those poor boys! They were such a funny combination of innocence and not knowing the rules for good behavior.

"No one will go to jail because you are going to do the right thing tomorrow," I told them. "One of the staff members will take you and the pajamas back to the store and you will tell the person in charge that you didn't know that what you did was stealing. Tell him that your housemother, Miss Edith, told you how bad it was and explained that we can't take anything out of a store unless you give money for it. Tell the truth and promise that you will never do it again."

Joe had apparently been standing outside our door listening to what I was telling the boys. He walked into the dorm and announced that he would take the boys to the store and help them return the clothes. He stuck around until everyone had settled down and gone to sleep. Then we went down to report to Father Curzon what had happened and received his approval for the way we handled it.

Just two days later, all the kids piled into the buses headed for a summer camp near Devil's Lake, Wisconsin. They were excited to be off to somewhere new, be able to go swimming and enjoy the outdoors. I was eager to go home to see my mother, but I also knew that Joe was staying at Lawrence Hall, and I had a room there if I wanted to visit.

The time off gave me space to think about the boys, and Joe and I spent time together discussing them and becoming even closer.

Third Life

COURTSHIP

Chapter 6

A DINNER GUEST

———

When I arrived home, my mother was glad to see me. I told her that I was tired and I wanted to spend the day napping and reading a new paperback I bought on the way home.

"Mama," I said, "you know that I love you and I will be a social person by supper time. If you would like to go out, I'll treat you. After all, I just got my first paycheck."

Mama just grinned and said, "Well, we won't spend it all in one place."

We spent the next couple of days reminiscing, catching up on family news, talking about my job, and discussing her health and possible retirement. She was sixty-six years old and still teaching. It concerned me. She seemed tired and not in the peak of health, but she was still energetic, so I wondered if I was imagining trouble that didn't exist.

I was sorting through some of my clothes to combine them with Mama's wash when the phone rang. Mama answered the call and held the receiver out to me.

"There's someone named Joe who wants to talk to you," she said. The expression on her face looked like she wanted to say, "Who on earth is Joe?"

I was very surprised to think that Joe had found our phone number and was calling, but it was a nice surprise. I wondered if something had changed at Lawrence Hall. Taking the phone from her hand, I gave her a big smile, then said, "Hello, Joe, what's up?"

"Good to hear your voice," Joe replied from the other end. "I just got back from class and I have the rest of the day off. Since it's only noon now, I was wondering if I could come to Downers Grove to see you and meet your mother?"

"Sounds like a plan to me but wait a second so I can get the train schedule," I replied, quickly locating the paper with the Burlington Northern train times on it from downtown Chicago to Downers Grove. "Take the El train or a bus to the Loop and go to Union Station on Canal Street. Tell the driver you want to go to Union Station because he will tell you if you need a transfer and where to get off. Once you are in the station, go to the area where the Burlington trains depart. There is a train that leaves at 2:20 and gets to Downers at 3:05, and I will meet you at the spot where the train stops and you get off. Did you get all that?"

"Yeah, I took notes. See you soon," he replied, and we both hung up the phone.

My mother had been listening with a straight face, but a twinkle in her eyes. "And just who is this Joe?" she asked.

"He maintains the kitchen at the Hall," I replied. "In the morning he goes to college to complete a degree in electrical engineering. He has been very helpful to me and oriented me to living there. He has many interesting stories about his time as an army medic in Italy, and he is on GI bill status which pays his college expenses."

At three o'clock I was at the station, waiting for the train to pull in. I saw Joe arrive. He walked up the platform carrying a small house plant which was in full bloom. It was obvious he wanted to hug me, but the plant kept his hand engaged and it was a bit awkward. However, he managed to hang on to the plant with one hand and hold my hand as we walked the two blocks to my home.

Mama was seated in the living room and rose as we entered the house. I made the introductions and Joe said, "I'm very pleased to meet you. Here is a little something to remember me by." Then he handed her the flowering plant. She looked surprised and smiled. She stood still for a few seconds, looking him over, and then thanked him. I thought he was pretty clever and mama appreciated the gesture. We all sat down together.

"It's getting close to four o'clock, and we usually have supper by six; Joe, how would you like to join us for supper?" Mama asked. "We'd be delighted to have you, and there are evening trains you can catch that leave after eight."

"Thank you, Mrs. King, I would like that very much," Joe replied.

"Alright then, I'll leave you two alone and go to the kitchen to see what I can cook. I'll let you know when to come to the table." She left, taking Joe's plant with her.

Joe and I were sitting on the sofa when he moved closer to me and put his arm around my shoulder. I relaxed and he pulled me even closer. I snuggled and put my head on his chest. Neither one of us spoke; we just enjoyed the moment. It was then I began to question if I might really allow myself to fall in love with him.

Now Edith be careful, you still don't know very much about Joe. Time to find out what you don't know.

I pushed myself into an upright sitting position and said to Joe, "I want to know your last name, where you were born and raised, and all about your family. I can tell from your slight accent that you probably grew up in or near New England."

"Edith, I knew that you were very intelligent, but you put it to work," he replied, smiling at me. "OK, I, Joseph F. Vosefski, just told you my name. We pronounce it VO chef ski. That's an Ellis Island spelling. My grandfather didn't know any English when he came, and the immigration agent didn't know any Polish, so this is the legal spelling for my family. And the accent is on the second syllable. My grandfather was a coal miner and married a Polish girl who had been living here for two years before him. They named their son Stanislav and he became my father. Dad had first and second grade formal education and then went into the mines to work when he turned eight. He married Stella and had six children. I had two older brothers and a sister, I was next, then two younger brothers.

"My oldest brother was Stash, who grew up to be a Merchant Marine. Next came

Lenny, who was a Marine, killed at Guadalcanal in WWII. My sister, Eleanor was the only daughter; then I was born. My younger siblings are John, another Marine and college graduate with Uncle Sam paying his tuition, and Robert, the youngest who is also a Marine with PTSD. Unfortunately, he was in and out of Veteran Hospitals and never really found his right place in the world. John had ambition and worked as a fireman which was his training in the Marines and started working on college credits until he finally had a master's degree in fire science. He became The Fire Chief of Escondido, married and had a son and a daughter.

"My parents were very loving parents and they were determined that all of their children would finish high school with a diploma. We did that. But I was extremely proud of my father, who managed to learn to read English and Polish and kept up with the news."

He paused and took a breath.

"Edith, I'd like to stop talking about my family for now and ask you about yours."

"Fair enough. There is so much to share, I don't know where to start," I replied. "What are you most curious about?"

"I'd like to know about your father. You've never mentioned him."

I breathed a deep sigh. I told him the whole heart-wrenching story of how dad had been killed by a drunk driver who ran a stop sign miles from home, how he was taken to the local hospital, and how my sister and I took the train to see him a day later, just before he died. My voice was getting softer the longer I talked, and tears streamed down my cheeks, as I began to sob rather loudly.

Joe immediately took me in his arms to comfort me, and my mother came rushing into the room to see why I was crying so hard. She had a slightly angry expression and asked me what happened. Her face made me think she was making sure that Joe hadn't made me cry. When I was able to catch my breath, I told her that I had just told Joe about Dad's fatal accident. She looked relieved.

"Why don't you come to the kitchen and wash your face," she suggested. "Joe can use the bathroom if he needs it and wash his hands because dinner will be ready soon."

Mama had already set the table with Joe's flowers in the middle. We stood behind our chairs until Mama said grace, then Joe pulled out her chair and seated her. I guess I'm not the only one with Victorian manners, I thought,

I was a bit subdued, so I asked Joe to tell Mama some of the interesting stories from his army days in Italy. First, he looked at Mama and asked, "Is that a topic that will interest you?" She nodded yes, and the evening was off to an entertaining start.

"Well, I was stationed in the Italian Alps, north of Trieste on the border of Yugoslavia, when Tito was threatening to invade in order to capture the port of Trieste from the Italians," Joe began. "I was a medic who helped the Major who was the doctor. I was in charge of the bi- weekly check-up of the prostitutes and handing out condoms but I became a surgical assistant. The people in the area were born without a doctor and died without one also."

Joe told us that one day he found himself all alone in the medical building--even the Major was gone-- when he heard a screaming baby and went to see what happened. He found a frantic mother with a badly burned, 14-month-old baby in her arms. She told Joe the baby had reached up onto the stove, touched a pan of boiling water and dumped it on herself. The mother had wrapped her daughter in a soft blanket and carried her a half mile to get to the medical facility. Joe treated her wounds and told her to come back the next day so that the Major could check the baby. Then he called the guys in the motor pool to drive the mother and her baby back to their village. The next day about a third of the village returned with the mother and her baby. None of them had ever been to a doctor and they either had a complaint or wanted to see what a doctor looked like. The Major, who was very compassionate to the people, said that since Joe had done such a good job and he could speak simple Italian, that he could go to the village for a half day every week to help the people who had never seen a doctor. It was unauthorized, but it was the right thing to do.

Joe told us other stories too, but soon it was seven-twenty and almost time for him to head for the train. We rose from the table.

"Wait one minute please," he said. He stood up, walked over to my mother and stood at attention as though he was addressing a high-ranking general.

"Mrs. King, I wish to inform you that I am deeply in love with your daughter and plan to marry her. I hope you will give us your blessing."

Mama shifted her eyes and glanced at me. I was completely amazed! I never expected him to say anything like that. He never asked me to marry him. I barely shook my head no, hoping Joe did not see, and hoping my mother did. Luckily, she saw.

"Joe, bless you, I like you very much, but I am waiting to hear more about your family," she said matter-of-factly. "Now, you need to leave for the train. But you need to cross the tracks because the trains going to Chicago leave on the other side of the platform. Thanks for coming, and I'll see you soon and may God go with you until we meet again," she said.

We said our goodbyes and I found myself looking out a window, watching Joe leave. He was on his way to the train, but it seemed as though it was the wrong direction because he was going away from me. As I watched him, I could feel Mama's eyes on me. I knew I had a lot of explaining to do.

Chapter 7

MUCH TO THINK ABOUT

Once we were alone, the cross examination began. Mama wanted more details about Joe. "This certainly isn't the evening that I expected," she said.

"Neither did I. But even though it was unusual, what did you think of him?" I replied.

"He seems to be a nice person, funny, caring, and quite intelligent. How come you didn't know his last name?"

"When anyone would ask him, he'd say you couldn't pronounce it, so just call me Joe." It was obvious that there was a lot more to know about Joe.

The month of July was very active. I enjoyed catching up with my friend Arden and discovered she had just received an engagement ring. A few days later, Arden brought Vince over to introduce him and tell us that they were engaged.

I was not impressed. I thought he was a jerk. My mother said to me, "Oh I hope Arden comes to her senses. That is not the right person for her."

A couple of weeks later, Arden came to see my mother. She was by herself and wanted to talk with her. We had known her for many years and she really admired my family and often expressed affection for my mother.

She told Mama that she had told Vince that she couldn't marry him and that she tried to give his ring back to him and he would not accept it. She continued to have a long talk about marriage and ultimately, Mama told her she was right to trust her instincts. Arden kept that advice. She took her ring off and asked her father to return it to Vince.

I admit that I missed Joe, so I decided to return to Lawrence Hall. Joe was very attentive, and we acted more like a dating couple. He didn't mention marriage again.

When I asked him about his early childhood, I heard another example of how clever he was. In the middle of the Great Depression, when he was eight years old, he started his own business. He lived in the Pocono Mountain district of Pennsylvania. The surrounding area was covered with coal mines and most of the mines were deep underground and did not disturb the beauty of the landscape.

However, there were also some spots where strip mining had begun and then was abandoned because it wasn't productive enough. Joe figured out that if he got a large bucket, he could collect the lumps of coal and take them home for the coal-burning stove his family used for cooking and heating their home. It turned out to be so useful that he began to sell coal to the neighbors. He charged an amount that everyone could afford but was less than what a coal delivery cost.

In addition to the coal business, during berry season the hills were filled with many different berry bushes. He would pick a variety of different berries in large quantities and his mother would produce jelly or jam from them, so they could have enough for many months.

* * * * *

While I was at Northwestern, I met a woman named Judith, who was about four years older than me. She was a guest one Sunday at Canterbury Club, the organization for Episcopal students that I attended regularly. Non-students could not join but could attend as guests. We became good friends, but Father Maxwell told her that regular attendance was limited to students and she needed to find a church where she could make friends. Judith suggested that we attend St. Luke's Episcopal Church together.

At that time, the Episcopal Church was presented in different parishes in very different ways. Some had a service of morning prayer on Sunday that reflected the absence of the Pope. St. Luke's in Evanston was very similar to traditional Catholic churches where you experienced chants and multiple masses. I loved it, and thought it was very much like the Roman Catholic church that Joe once served as an altar boy when he was growing up.

I called Judith, "Jude." She was employed as a writer for

the Chicago Tribune. She sometimes worked as a reporter, but most of her job was social news about well-off people, or a cute story about a child, or maybe even a special dog. We both had lost our fathers at an early age, so she jokingly said that we were "sisters of the double-cross." We had fun planning an agenda for our "order" of sisters who had been given a bad deal in life, but in reality, it also helped us plan our daily devotions.

Of course, I was destined to introduce her to Joe, and Joe and I took the "L" north to Howard Street, which was only a block or so to Juneway Terrace where Jude lived with her grandparents and her mother. We decided to go to a nearby restaurant that was within walking distance and settled in for the evening. We had snacks for food, and Joe and Jude matched each other in drinks. I stuck to 7-up, but Jude had a few fancy cocktails. I don't remember what Joe had, but I remember it was very strong.

About ten-thirty in the evening, we walked Jude home, but she was just plain drunk. She was stumbling and needed help walking. Joe helped her up the steps and once through the door, he picked her up and carried her to her bedroom. I told Joe to go back to Lawrence Hall and I would see she got to bed safely. But I ended up spending the night with her.

It was one of the strangest nights of my life. Fortunately, her family had gone to bed early. Trying to keep her quiet was the hardest part. After she laid down, she started muttering on her bed. She said crazy things like, "hold me down or the ceiling is gonna get me." "the room is twirling and turning," and "hold on to me so I don't fly away," etc. I laid down next to her, put my arm across her middle, and softly sang some Irish and Scottish lullabies to her. Soon after, she was asleep and so was I.

Little did I suspect that years later, she would go on to marry a priest. Hallelujah!

The next morning, I returned to the Hall. I was quite tired as I had not slept well the night before. I went to my bedroom and laid down for a nap, fully dressed in yesterday's clothes. I slept for several hours until I was awakened by a loud knock on my door.

"Who is it?" I called out, knowing the door was unlocked.

"It's Joe."

"Come in."

I didn't bother to get up. The door opened and Joe entered, his face contorted in a look of great sadness and tears. My body tensed, waiting for him to say something terrible. He looked around and said, "Dammit, there aren't any chairs in this room, and I need to talk to you."

"Alright, since you obviously want privacy, this room is where you can get it," I replied, apprehensively. "You have two choices. You can sit on the bed with me or you can lie down next to me and I'll listen to whatever you have to say."

I put on my mental suit of calm, but I was afraid of what I was going to hear. He grabbed a tissue, wiped his face and laid beside me. For a couple minutes, he just laid still, taking deep breaths to calm himself. My right hand slowly wandered over to his left hand, and he found his voice.

"Oh Edie, I was just starting to write a letter to my mother, when Dewey came to tell me there was a long distance call for me from Pennsylvania. My brother John called to tell me that my mother is so sick that they took her to the hospital two days ago, and they amputated her right leg above the knee today and they are praying for her life," he said. He began to moan a little as he tried to catch his breath.

"She has had diabetes for years and took care of it until my brother Leonard was killed at Guadalcanal in the early part of World War II. He was a Marine, and my mom was sitting in the kitchen one day when she let out a scream and started to cry. Those of us who were home rushed in to see what had happened. She was shaking and said, 'Lennie just died!' We tried to convince her that there was no way she could know that, but about six weeks later we got the official notice of his dying in action and his purple heart. Her psychic ability was right on target. He died the day she felt it. Little by little, she became more and more depressed and when I came home from Italy, I started giving her the insulin shots she needed. And I taught my sister how to do it too. Maybe I should have never left her. But then I would never have met you."

"May God help you, darling!" I cried.

I rolled over on my side and embraced him and we

shared a passionate kiss. I immediately rolled off the bed and suggested that we both sit on the edge of the bed with our feet on the floor.

As Joe sat down beside me, with a smile that was as broad as his face, he said, "Did I just hear you call me darling?"

I smiled back, with a smile as big as his. "Yes, you did. I just discovered that I really am in love with you."

"I am so happy that we are on the same page at last, and now is the right moment to tell you something that I have kept to myself ever since the day you came for your interview," he began. "Just after you left the kitchen, I was thinking about how beautiful you are, and how sweet you must be to apply for this kind of job. When all of a sudden, I seemed to be standing in a shaft of bright light and I heard a voice in my head say, 'You have found your MATE.' It scared me and I wondered if I was going crazy. I felt rooted to the ground and just kept standing there, wondering. Then Dewey reentered the kitchen, sort of stared at me and said, 'what's up?' I told him 'I am going to marry that girl.' Dewey blinked his eyes a couple of times, shook his head in disbelief, and walked out of the kitchen."

"After much thought and a bit of prayer, I decided that it must have been a message from heaven, but I found it hard to believe. I kept it from you because I thought you would think I was nuts or trying to manipulate you. But I accept it as a precious gift now."

"And so will I. Thanks be to God," I said.

Chapter 8

A LOOK TO THE FUTURE

"Joe, do you want to fly home to see your mother?" I asked.

"No, I can't, flying is too expensive," he replied, sadly. I felt sorry for him because I knew how much he wanted to go home and comfort his mother after her amputation.

"I might be able to help you with that. I have a savings account and it may have enough to pay for a flight," I offered. "You can have it."

"No thanks, that just isn't right. You shouldn't have to pay for it," he replied.

Smiling, I answered, "Why not? Isn't she going to be my mother-in-law? Or have you decided that you are through with me?"

Joe looked at me in amazement. "Please, don't think like that. We're going to be together forever," he said.

"I know, so you could start thinking of me as part of your family," I stated, matter-of-factly, "and I think that you should send your mother some flowers. There is a flower shop down the street a couple of blocks east of here, and they can telegraph the shop nearest the hospital and deliver them. Tell them what to write on the card and make it something that will show your mother that you love her. Ok?"

"Wow, you know many things I don't know," he replied, "and I love the fact that you are willing to teach me."

"That's because I think like a woman, and I know what impresses one," I answered. "How about giving me a goodbye kiss when you go? I need to get out of these clothes I've been wearing for two days and take a shower. And I look forward to you coming back soon."

I fussed about in the bathroom for a long time, washing my hair, putting on makeup, doing everything to look spectacular. Then I went to my closet to pick out a dress that was a little sexy. I chose my black and white, cotton dress with the short-sleeves, tight waistline and low, but not too low, neckline. I went back into the bathroom, where there was a full-length mirror on the door, and I passed inspection. When I opened the door to return to the bedroom, there were two chairs there and Joseph was sitting in one of them looking smug.

I pointed to the unoccupied chair and said, "Great. Thanks, you're quite an operator."

"Don't mention it. You're looking very gorgeous, and I can provide you with just the right lap to sit on," he said.

"I see, you had ulterior motives when you brought these chairs, well good for you. You know how to think." I accepted his invitation. But it was short lived, because it was his night to cook again.

Soon our time together would be cut short as we were both getting ready to resume our full-time schedules. Time seemed to be racing, and the students returned from camp. They had many wonderful stories to tell. They bragged about what they had learned and asked if we had any books about the wild animals they had seen. Since they were now familiar with me, the job seemed to be easier, but Joe and I had less time together.

One day, Joe asked me how many boyfriends I had had before we met. The answer was "not many."

"How can that be? I'm not sure I believe that," he said. "What was the matter with the guys you had at your schools? Were they blind? You're so gorgeous. It doesn't make sense."

"Well, I did date some, but I was so much more mature than most of the boys and I was also an honor student, and sometimes referred to as 'The Brain.' You need to remember these were boys, nothing like the man you are," I told him. Then I added playfully, "I'm feeling a bit insulted by you saying you aren't sure you believe me. If you are trying to find out if I have had a lover, the answer is NO." Then I turned serious. "I was brought up to believe that the use of my body was to be my gift to my husband," I continued. "In fact, the marriage vows used to include this phrase. 'I thee with my body shall worship.' I'm really rattled by your doubt. What have I done to cause it?"

"Oh Edie, I'm so sorry. It's because you are such an expert kisser, and you do some things that are so great, I just got to thinking and wondering where you learned all that," he replied, sheepishly.

I burst into gales of laughter and decided to tell him the story.

"Well, if I tell you the absolute truth, you may have trouble believing it, but you better believe it, because it's rather typical of my way of thinking. I had a sociology class in college in which we were studying various indigenous tribes and cultures. I chose a reference on making love, written about three thousand years ago in Sanskrit. It was used for instructing the upper caste people to make love in all sorts of ways that are usually not known in the western part of the world. The book was called The Kama Sutra. Frankly, I don't really remember most of what it said, but it inspired me to decide that when I found my forever love, I'd use my imagination and become an expert at lovemaking. Is it clear to you that I have saved myself for you, and do you like the idea?"

"Well, I have heard that some wedding nights are rather unpleasant if the bride is inexperienced. I don't want to ever hurt you," he replied.

"My goodness, Joseph, you are such a dear sweet soul," I said, deeply touched. "Besides, for centuries it has been called deflowering. Anything like that can't be all bad. It's so natural and necessary to get the process started. I worry more about whether I need to get a sexy night gown. My friend Jude said, 'If I had enough money to do it, I would give you a custom-made night gown with fur around the bottom, so it could keep your neck warm in the winter.'"

With twinkling eyes and a chuckle, Joe said, "I see that Jude is still being creative. Sounds like a good idea; I bet she could market it."

We both had a good laugh over that.

* * * * *

In August, the boys returned and there was much to do. We had to see that they were all properly enrolled in school. Some of the them had to have certain shots required by the school, and we had to take them to the doctor. The days just seemed to fly by. And our romance was progressing nicely too!

On the twenty-fourth of September, I received some shocking news. Joe came home from school and told me that a large number of students from his college, the American Television Institute & Electronic Engineering School, had dropped out or failed and would not be returning to school. As a result, the school suggested that the students in the junior class take a long vacation during November and December and the class behind them was entered into an accelerated program to catch up so that the two classes could be combined. The senior classes would not start until mid-January.

"You know, that would make a nice time to have a wedding," Joe hinted. "I know that you were planning a longer engagement, but I think that we should announce our plan to marry and talk to Father Curzon and see if he would marry us, so we can set the date."

"I am stunned. That's only weeks away!" I exclaimed. I was running my fingers through my hair, and caressing my hands, trying to get a grip on what I had just heard him say. Then, I was suddenly calm and knew it was the right thing to do. "Joe, why don't you go down to Father's office and tell him about the changed schedule and that we have agreed to be married. I'll be there in a minute or two, but I need a moment of silence first." I needed to let this all sink in.

Without a word, Joe hugged me as if he was never going to let go, then quickly kissed me, and left.

Pondering all sorts of possibilities, I slowly walked down the stairs and almost collided with Mrs. Curzon standing near the bottom step. I apologized for being inattentive and making her move quickly out of the way.

"Edith, you look worried," she said. "Is something wrong? If you need a friend, I volunteer."

"Thank you, Mrs. Curzon," I replied. "Joe and I are about to meet in Father's office, and I would welcome your presence with us."

She immediately hooked her arm through mine and we walked together to the office.

Inside, we were cordially greeted and asked to sit down.

The two men took turns summarizing what they had talked about. Mrs. Curzon asked Joe, "Why are you in such a hurry? Planning a wedding takes more than a few weeks."

Joe answered her question with great passion as he spoke. "If we married in November, I would be able to be a very attentive husband because I would no longer have hours of studying. Of course, I would still be doing the kitchen and other jobs here, but I hope I could help Edith in the dorm. I know that when my class starts in January, I will be very busy for the rest of next year. In addition to my classes, I will have to research a new theory and write a dissertation on it. I just think that we would be off to a better start if we had a couple of less complicated months."

I loved what I had just heard. I asked Father C. if he would marry us in the chapel at Lawrence Hall, and he consented and asked what date we wanted to hold the ceremony. Mrs. C. reached for a calendar and said, "November first is a feast day. It's All Saint's Day and this year it's on a Saturday. Does that interest you?"

I looked at Joe and shook my head yes. He looked very happy as he nodded in agreement. Father C. advised us to ask his wife to help with the planning, saying she had much experience, and enjoyed doing it.

That same afternoon, the school bus arrived, and the kids came storming in, so Joe took my hand and escorted me up to the dorm. He motioned for the kids to go in first, leaving us alone in the hallway at the top of the stairs.

"Sorry we can't talk now, but I'll be as fast as I can to get out of the kitchen early tonight," he promised. "What a crazy day this has been. But I'm so happy." He planted a quick kiss on my lips, then went down the stairs.   A s soon as I walked into the dorm, one of the boys appeared, whose name was Danny.

"How come you and Joe were kissing out in the hall?" he inquired in an obnoxiously loud voice.

"Danny, that question is asking for information that is private and not really any of your business," I replied coolly. "I'm telling this to you and all of the boys; that kind of question is not a good question to ask. However, I am willing to give you an honest answer. We love each other, and we will be having a wedding soon.

Right now, let's play a game until it's time for dinner. But first, let's take five minutes for you to hang up your coat and go to the bathroom if you need to."

After the boys were settled again, I told them to sit on the floor and form a circle. I sat down with them.

"The game I'm going to show you is called, *I'm going to London and I'm going to take a blank.* You will take turns saying what you will take. This game will help you to remember things you hear and learn to remember a series of words," I explained.

"Now, let's do a little practice run, so everyone will understand what to do," I continued. "I will say the sentence and you call out the word. *I am going to London and I'm going to take a .."*

"Cat!" cried Johnny.

I smiled kindly at him. "That's a fun answer, but do you think you could take a cat in a suitcase? Let's try another word."

This was rather difficult for many of the boys, which is why I wanted to see if they were ready for it. They came up with so many ridiculous things that they enjoyed it. Being silly is fun, and it took my mind off of the serious things I would have to decide very soon. Dorm one was in a joyful mood when we entered the dining room.

Fourth Life

MARRIAGE

Chapter 9

MAKING QUICK PLANS

———

Later, after dinner, and when the kids were in bed, Joe and I called my mother to tell her that we were engaged.

"Mama, I have a surprise for you," I said to her when she answered the phone. "Joe and I are going to get married."

"That's no surprise," she said. She had a feeling that Joe was the right person for me. But she was also amazed at the timing. "Edith don't you know that four weeks is not enough notice?"

"Yes, I'm sure everyone we invite will wonder about it, but I want to assure you that there is no embarrassing explanation needed," I replied. "I'm still a 'good girl.' Joe's school is the one to blame."

"Glad to hear that, but I really didn't expect anything else."

"Oh, Mama, I love you! You're always so nice," I said. "Can you see to getting the invitations printed? It's too late for an engraved one, and the printers make some really nice printed ones. Pick whatever strikes your fancy. After all, a woman who earned her degree from the University of Chicago has good enough judgment to choose the right invitation for her daughter, a mere graduate of Northwestern University." We always teased each other about our alma maters.

My mother chuckled and said, "You are exactly right. Glad to be of service. Are you going to have an engagement ring, or just a wedding ring?"

"I'm not sure we can afford one," I replied. "We can wait until we have full-time employment."

"Well, maybe Aunt Grace can help you out with that. She has a jeweler in Chicago," suggested my mother. "She says he is an old friend, and always gives her a discount. It won't hurt to ask her if he might consider helping her niece who is marrying a veteran currently in college on the GI Bill. He can't say yes unless we ask; we won't do it if Grace thinks it is not appropriate. Either Grace or I will call you back on that. However, explain why Joe's school is to blame for the rush."

I explained how Joe thought it would be a good idea to launch our marriage before he had to resume his studies. Mama seemed to understand.

"One more thing, Mama," I began, "I'd like to have Uncle Pat walk me down the aisle, and it seems to me that you should be the one to ask him. Does that seem right to you?" Aunt Grace and Uncle Pat were my father's brother and sister, and much-loved family. I was eagerly looking forward to seeing them both again. "Yes, I'll take care of it," she said quickly. "Now, this is going to be a busy month, but please take my advice and pace yourself. A groom does not want a worn-out bride. I'll let you go now and call me if you need anything else. God bless you. Good night."

Joe had been seated beside me and able to hear the conversation about getting a discount on a wedding ring. Once again, he said, "You amaze me. You're able to get a discount on a diamond?"

"Perhaps, we'll know by tomorrow. When is your next day off?" I asked.

"Saturday," he replied.

"Oh good, That's my day too."

"Maybe we could go to the Loop and look at rings?" Joe suggested. "You said that a diamond could wait and that a cheaper stone was acceptable, but whatever you pick I want a stone that sparkles like you do. Perhaps I shouldn't compare you to a diamond; they are really hard, where you are soft and cuddly."

"You just say the nicest things," I replied, smiling. "No wonder I love you so much!"

Standing up, Joe lifted me off my chair, hugged me to his body, and his soft lips found mine. We had a long intermission in our wedding planning session. It was becoming more difficult to be practical.

The next day, after the boys left for school, I went shopping for my wedding dress. I remembered seeing a wedding display in a store window, so I stopped there first. They told me that they had sold all of their collection, except for one in my size. They said it was for sale at a discount, because it had been modeled in a fashion show, and it was now considered second hand. I tried it on, and it fit perfectly. It covered my generous bosom and nipped in my waist. Beautiful lace cascaded over a full, ballerina-length skirt, and it had long lace sleeves. Having found a white dress, my next stop was Chandler's shoe store, where I bought white satin pumps. Then I hurried back to work.

When Mrs. Curzon saw me come in carrying a couple of packages, she asked, "Edith, did you have any luck finding what you wanted?"

"Yes, I found my wedding dress. It's beautiful lace and the store is going to deliver it tomorrow. I took the El to Evanston so I couldn't carry it myself."

"That's wonderful, I'm so happy for you," Mrs. Curzon replied, smiling.

"Well, I think I had better get back to work," I said. "I'm going to get a head start on the laundry because Joe and I both have Saturday off, and we are going to look at rings and possibly visit my mother."

As I entered the laundry room, I thought, *this must be the right place to be; after all, this is where our romance started.*

When Saturday arrived, Joe and I left for the Loop at eight-thirty in the morning. We were in a joyous mood as we arrived at the jewelry store that my Aunt Grace suggested. It was a small storefront in a high-rise building. The part open to the public was very small with a long showcase across the whole room. But there was a door that led to a larger jewelry showroom in the back. When we walked in, the manager greeted us with a handshake.

"My name is Edith, and I am Grace Powell's niece," I said. "This is my beloved, and his name is Joseph."

"I'm Mr. Johnson," he replied. "And yes, I had a nice chat with your aunt, and she told me that Joe was studying engineering on a GI Bill arrangement. My son is also a veteran. Where did you serve?"

"In Italy, during the occupation," Joe replied. They spent a minute or two talking about the military. Then we got down to business and the diamonds came out. They were beautiful, but I had to choose something in our price range. Mr. Johnson carefully picked out three rings, and after measuring my finger, I tried them on. I asked Joe if he liked any of them, and he pointed out the one I liked best. It had a yellow gold band and a larger round diamond that was considered almost a half carat in size. The diamond was nestled into the gold, instead of being mounted on high prongs. It made the ring look bigger, and also made me believe the diamond would stay put forever and ever, as it should.

The moment of truth had arrived; I had left the ring on my finger and put my hand on top of Joe's hand. He asked the price. It retailed for $350 but Mr. Johnson offered us an amazing discount. However, he had us pick out the plain, yellow gold wedding rings before he told us the unbelievable deal. Mr. Johnson gave us the final price plus twenty percent off all three rings, and we paid cash. I couldn't wait to show Mama.

We found a public phone and called her to see if we could visit. We were able

to catch the next train to Downers Grove, and we were feeling so elated that we splurged on a taxi to take us to the train station.

When we arrived at home, Mama had invited the neighbor ladies, Helen and Dorothy, to come and meet Joe. Since showing off my ring was the order of the day, we did that too. Mama had called Arden, and she came over about an hour after we arrived. I introduced Arden to Joe, and they sat down together to get to know each other while I conferred with Mama about wedding details. Arden offered to give me a wedding shower and we managed to find a date we could agree on.

About a week before the wedding, we all gathered for my shower. There were some friends from high school, from Northwestern, and even my sorority sisters. Arden had asked me what I wanted, and I told her I had no decent underwear or slips! I told her that everything under my clothes was rags. So I was dutifully showered with new fancy underwear, a beautiful night gown, a negligee, and things to replace my worn-out college clothing. Lucky me!

The first of November was rapidly approaching. I

called Father Maxwell, the priest who had presented me for Confirmation while I was a student at Northwestern University, to ask him if he would assist Father Curzon with my wedding. He accepted with delight, and I told him it was to be a morning wedding with a nuptial mass.

Since the wedding was small, so was the wedding party. Joe called a friend of his from the Milwaukee School of Engineering and asked him to be his best man. Unfortunately, he was busy that weekend, so Joe asked one of his coworkers from Lawrence Hall. His name was William Franklin Lane.

My sister Elizabeth was a clear choice for my maid of honor. We went shopping together and bought a green taffeta dress with a long-sleeved, little bolero jacket. that was suitable for the wedding but could be worn afterwards too.

Mrs. Curzon offered me the use of her wedding veil. The veil was attached to a small, Russian-style hat and it partially covered my face and hung down to my shoulders in the back.

One of our colleagues from Lawrence Hall even offered to take snapshots for us since we were not able to hire a photographer. After the event, he gave us a beautiful album to treasure.

Everything was ready for our wedding day, which was also All Saints Day, 1952. I felt good about everything, and following my mother's advice, I wasn't even worn out!

Chapter 10

A SACRED COVENANT

———

My Uncle Pat and his wife Carol drove from South Bend, Indiana the night before, which was Halloween. He picked up my mother and drove to Lawrence Hall for a rehearsal of the wedding. When we finished, we piled into his car and went out to a nearby restaurant which was having a Halloween celebration. We had a good time together, and Uncle Pat and Joe got into a deep conversation about cars, while we ladies talked about the wedding.

After dinner, Uncle Pat took me aside. "I have a very good impression of Joe," he said. "Your mother has told us a lot about him, and she is absolutely convinced that he is the right choice for you. Will his parents be here tomorrow?"

"Unfortunately, no. His mother has had one of her legs amputated, and she doesn't want to make the trip," I explained. "We will call her tomorrow and tell her and Joe's father all about the wedding. We will send some pictures when they are developed."

We returned to Lawrence Hall in my uncle's car. He

had the latest model Studebaker and everyone in America was talking about it. It was no wonder to us, because my uncle was C. A. King, the treasurer of the Studebaker Corporation. Pat was his nickname.

Joe and I said good night as soon as we returned, because I wanted to wash and set my hair. The next morning, I woke up about six-thirty and had a guest at seven. My friend Jude came in and announced that she was going to help me dress. She also combed my hair and styled it, but it was very simple. Then Mrs. Curzon came to my room and announced that she had finished making my bouquet. It was indeed lovely, and made of white roses, stephanotis, trailing small ivy, and baby's breath with pale blue ribbons. It was a gift from Mrs. Curzon. She had acquired the flowers from a florist and put it all together. Joe had bought an orchid corsage for me, and we placed it, along with my bouquet and the flowers for my sister to carry, in the refrigerator.

The ceremony was scheduled for ten o' clock in the morning, and my family arrived at Lawrence Hall at nine. My mother found Joe in the dining room in his old clothes, having a cup of coffee. She wondered what was going on and asked Joe if he needed any help. "No," he replied, "but I just realized that last night was the last night I could sleep in my underwear and I have to run down the block and buy some pajamas." And then he went out the door.

Then Mama and Lizzie came to my room and chatted for a few minutes, but they could see that Jude was the only helper I needed. So they went downstairs to the reception area.

A few minutes before ten, I went downstairs to discover a state of chaos. Father Maxwell had not arrived, and the flowers in the refrigerator were gone. Jude went to find Joe, who was being kept out of sight by Bill, a friend of Joe's from work who was serving as the best man. Joe was well acquainted with the refrigerator and rushed to see what he could do. Jude followed him. There had been an early morning delivery of eggs, and cartons of eggs were piled up to the ceiling of the refrigerator room. Joe removed several of the cartons and discovered the flowers. The bride's bouquet was okay, and the orchid was in a plastic box and unharmed. However, the maid of honor's flowers were completely crushed. So we decided that my sister would carry the orchid during the ceremony.

Minutes before the wedding started, the guests were filling the pews and Father Maxwell showed up. A lady who supplied music on Sundays began playing softly while the best man and the groom took their place near the altar.

Then, the wedding march filled the chapel with music and Lizzie started down the aisle. Next it was my turn, with Uncle Pat alongside me. I saw Joe standing at the front of the church waiting for me. We smiled at each other and he looked very happy.

As Father read from *The Book of Common Prayer*, in our very traditional ceremony, he asked Joe, "Joseph. will you have this woman to be your wife; to live together in the covenant of marriage? Will you love her, comfort her, honor her in sickness and in health, and forsaking all others, be faithful to her as long as you both shall live?"

"I will," answered Joe. I was asked the same question and agreed, and the wedding proceeded. When Joe took my hand, his hand had a strong tremor. As the wedding continued, his knees shook so badly that the wide skirt of my dress also began to shake.

At one point, Father Maxwell bent down to him and whispered, "Are you dizzy? Do you feel faint?' Joe silently shook his head no, took a couple of deep breaths, and the rest of the ceremony went smoothly. Afterwards, Father Maxwell told us that he had been so afraid that Joe was going to pass out. He said the brides never do, but he had seen grooms hit the floor.

After the closing kiss, the pianist began playing Greensleeves and we walked up the aisle, elated. I felt like I could fly. However, I had to put the brakes on when I noticed Arden and a strange man sitting on the edge of the aisle. I asked Joe to stop. Arden slipped out of the pew and gave me a big hug. The guy with her stood up and Arden turned toward him and said, "Edith and Joe, I want to introduce you both to John Schilb, my fiance." She held out her left hand. "John gave this to me last night," she said. On her third finger was a lovely marquise cut diamond set in white gold.

I was stunned. It had been only two months since she

cancelled her engagement to Vince. I had a dozen questions I wanted to ask right there, but now was not the right time. So we walked together to the reception area where the guests were gathering. Later on, I asked Arden how long she really had known John, and she laughed and told me that she had analyzed his urine at Argonne National Laboratory, where they both worked, for many years before she found out who it belonged to!

The reception was simple and attended by about forty people. We had little cream puffs filled with chicken salad, and small sandwiches, assorted mints, punch, and a lovely wedding cake topped with lovely wedding bells. Arden liked it so much, she made her father go to the same bakery for her own wedding cake. After an hour, the guests began to leave, and Joe and I excused ourselves to get into our travel clothes. My mother had arranged a brunch reception for the immediate family. It was in a very special restaurant in Evanston with good food and excellent service. As most of the people who were attending had driven their own cars, there was room for those who had arrived on public transportation to join the group and ride to Evanston. Arden, of course, had been invited, but we needed to add an extra place setting for her surprise fiancée.

Joe wore the suit he had on for the wedding so that he could make sure that Aunt Grace recognized the tie he was wearing. It was a shower gift for Joe. She had wrapped it very nicely and given it to me when Arden had the shower for me, but it was for Joe. When he opened it, there was a handsome, muted red silk tie with a raised blue dot in the center. He was impressed and pleased. He had never had a silk tie before.

We all obviously enjoyed ourselves. Four of my aunts were there, three of my mama's friends who dated back to her college days, and one uncle, plus some cousins and Arden and John. So there were seventeen in all. My mother suggested where people should sit, and after all were seated and engaged in conversation, there was a young man standing that she had never seen before. She looked at him and asked, "Who are you?"

"I'm from Lawrence Hall," he replied. "I stood out in the hallway and watched the wedding. I just wanted to come and see the rest of it because Joe was so special to me. I got put in Lawrence Hall instead of going to jail and Joe helped more than anyone and I wanted to see how happy he was."

"Well, I guess I better order another chair and another place setting, and you can sit next to me," my mother replied.

Joe was on the other end of the table, surrounded and monopolized by my old aunts. Later, he asked why the man was there and I told him what Mama said. "I had no idea he cared so much," he replied.

When the meal was done, we drove back to Lawrence Hall with my Mama in my uncle's car, where we got out and said our goodbyes and thanks. They drove my Mama to Downers Grove before returning to Indiana.

Dewey had promised us to drive us to the hotel we had booked in Chicago, and we arrived there about four o'clock. We were both so tired that we decided to take a nap and were asleep in less than a minute.

We woke up at six o'clock in the evening and Joe got up to call the restaurant which had been recommended to us. They confirmed that a reservation had already been made for us and they wanted to know if seven was too early. We said we'd be there and got ready to go.

The restaurant we spent our first meal alone together as a married couple was named Chez Paul. If you have ever seen the movie *The Blues Brothers*, you have seen Chez Paul. I don't know what it looks like now, or if it still exists, but the movie pictured it as it was on our wedding day. It was elegant and the service was excellent. We were impressed and felt like royalty. Joe and I had some fun making jokes about being royals, and we wondered where we had left our crowns, and if our carriage was awaiting us outside. I was glad to discover that Joe was capable of being silly with me, because I like people who can have a little fun being silly.

When it was time to pay the bill, the maître d' came to our table and handed Joe a check. He congratulated us and wished us a happy marriage. The check was for $0.00, and the message said," "Compliments of Mr. Randolf of the Wisconsin Hotel Association!" He was a contributor to

Lawrence Hall and had been on their board of directors. He had also covered our hotel as a wedding gift. We were in really high spirits and most grateful.

After dinner, Joe wanted to stop at a Walgreens to buy the early edition of the Sunday Tribune. When we got back to the hotel, he hung his jacket, sat down in a comfortable chair and started reading the newspaper. So I found a women's magazine and started reading. A considerable amount of time passed and neither one of us spoke. At first, I was just puzzled. Then a horrible thought entered my mind. What if he had decided that he really didn't want to be married, and if the marriage wasn't consummated, it would be easier to annul? What a terrible thought!!!

I grabbed my suitcase, took it into the bathroom with me, took a shower, then opened my suitcase and put on my fancy nightgown and negligee. I quietly walked up to Joe, who was still behind the newspaper. I wanted to tear the paper out of his hand, but I told myself that was no way to start a marriage. Instead, I gently put my hand over the top of the page he was holding and surprise, surprise, it woke him up.

"Are you going to read all night?" I asked, sweetly.

He dropped the paper, looked delighted, and pulled me onto his lap. I guess he did really want to be married after all!

Chapter 11

DESTINATION MILWAUKEE

After a most delightful night, we were both so happy and filled with joy that we marveled at the depth of our happiness. We had an early breakfast and boarded a train to Milwaukee. Since we only had three days off, we had picked a city that was nearby. It was also a place where Joe had lived for a year, when he attended the Milwaukee School of Engineering.

When we checked into our hotel, we were in an ordinary room, not a honeymoon suite. We checked the mattress and found it was fine for our purposes.

The morning was passing rapidly when Joe asked, "Edie, are you feeling up to going for a walk?"

"Sure, where do we want to go?" I replied.

"Did I ever tell you about the job I had when I lived here? Since I had been a medic, it made it easy for me to get a job in a nursing home. It was a well-run place and many of the patients were happy there. I'd like to visit and see if any of my employee friends are still working there. It will give me a chance to show you off. I'm just so proud that you are my wife. They'll take one look at you and envy me."

"Are you telling me that I've turned you into a big shot?" I raised my eyebrows and a smirk appeared, then turned into a smile.

"I've already figured out something about living with you," he replied. "Your sense of humor is so ubiquitous, that you are never going to be boring. You make life fascinating and fun. Is ubiquitous the right word? I didn't know I ever knew it, it just popped out and seemed right."

"Yes, my darling, give yourself credit for a good vocabulary. If you keep on learning new words, you may never know what genius you might impress and work with someday," I said. "I treasure the compliments you give me. You are truly a blessing. But didn't this conversation start with a question about going out for a walk?"

"Yeah, I got distracted," he said. "Get your coat and let's go."

We started down Wisconsin Avenue, heading toward Lake Michigan. We passed Marquette University, an assortment of various stores and businesses, and when we turned onto another street going north, we came upon a theater that startled us. The marquee featured a burlesque show.

"Look at that," I said to Joe "I didn't know that burlesque still existed. I thought it went away when Vaudeville died. Of course, being a small-town girl, I never saw such a show. Did you?"

"No, we didn't have any of that where I grew up," Joe admitted. "Do I detect a little curiosity in your question?"

"You read my mind," I replied. "If the tickets are cheap enough, I'd like to see what the show is all about. The only person I've ever heard of is Gypsy Rose Lee, but some of the comedians who are on the radio used to do standup in burlesque."

"Okay, I'll see about the tickets and when the show starts," said Joe. He stepped up to the box office and found out that the curtain was rising in fifteen minutes and the tickets were reduced on Monday to a dollar each, so we took a chance. The show was both interesting and funny. The comedians were good, and the ladies were talented and made removing most of their veils and fluffy feathers most intriguing. I was the only woman in the audience, and I clung to Joe's hand throughout the show. I was a little uneasy being surrounded by a theater full of men. Now that I know what burlesque is all about, I never need to see it again.

It was getting too late to visit the nursing home, so we decided to go to dinner. Joe was very excited to tell me about the restaurant he chose.

"Edie, we are headed for one of Milwaukee's top restaurants," he told me. "It's on Mason Street, which is in the heart of a very posh district. The Karl Ratzsch restaurant is so spectacular, you feel as if you are in Germany when you step through the door!" The walls are decorated with shelves of beautiful, cased crystal glassware. Many of the exhibits are from sovereign principalities that existed before Germany became a united country, and they're decorated with coats of arms, lots of gold, emeralds, rubies, and diamonds. I could go on and on, but you'll see it in a few minutes."

"Sounds like a museum with good food," I concluded. "Once again you have surprised me with your knowledge of fine glass. Where did you learn all that?" I said.

"When I was in the army, I had a leave for two weeks, and I went to Switzerland where I visited museums, restaurants, and shops," Joe began. "One day I wandered into a shop with a glass department. There were no customers in that department when I entered, and a gray-haired woman asked if she could show me anything. She spoke German, and I assumed she offered to wait on me, so I answered in English. She switched to English instantly. I admired the merchandise and asked her to explain something. Well, that opened the floodgate to her vast knowledge, and I spent almost an hour with her, taking me around to different types of glass and she gave me all sorts of information that my engineering mind could appreciate. Here we are, at the corner of Mason Street and Ratzsch's is right there."

I knew the moment we entered that Joe had not exaggerated. Not only was the décor very vivid but the aroma of the cooking was heavenly. We were seated where we had a view of most of the first floor. We ordered cream of mushroom soup, and it was so special. I experimented for years afterwards to try to get mine to taste like theirs. We had wiener schnitzel with dumplings and fresh vegetables. Schaum torte was dessert. I eventually learned to make schaum torte and impressed my family and friends. First, I would make a meringue so stiff that it could be shaped into a bowl with sides about an inch and a half high and about three inches in diameter. Then you fill the torte with quality vanilla ice cream, pour either thick chocolate or caramel sauce over it, apply whipped cream, and top with fresh berries of your choice. Yum. After that we were so full, we splurged on a taxi to take us back to the hotel. That evening, while we were still digesting our marvelous meal, we began to talk about making plans about how we wanted to be treated if we were ready to pick a fight.

"I can't imagine being very angry with you," I said to Joe, "but let's be realistic and share our reactions to anger. I hate to be yelled at. Most of the time that shuts me off and I don't respond. Occasionally, I raise my voice and tell whoever I'm fighting with to back off, and I'm walking away from them until we recover our senses and talk to each other like grownups. I've found this method works and doesn't even demand an apology."

Joe looked at me with a smile. "That's a really good way to handle anger," he said. "It enables you to stop the problem before you both get out of hand and then you can treat the other person with respect. You know, you are pretty clever. I can agree to plan fighting using our model. But that's enough talk for now." And he stopped me with a passionate kiss.

The next morning was Tuesday and the election day for President Dwight D. Eisenhower. We were both registered voters, but since we were not in our own district, we could not cast a ballot. It was the only national election I ever missed. I became a much more responsible citizen as I matured.

We took a bus and managed to visit Joe's friends at the nursing home. I heard some very nice things said about him. We finished our visit by ten thirty in the morning and decided to go back to the hotel. On the way, we stopped at a deli and bought some snacks.

"You know, we just bought so much food that it gave me an idea," Joe said. "Getting around this town without a car is not easy, and unless you have some more sightseeing in mind, I want to know if you might consider going back to Chicago this afternoon. We could check out before noon and I think we will not have to pay for another day. If you like the idea, let's check the train schedule in your purse and see if this could work."

"I like the idea, but I would like to go all the way to Downers Grove and spend the night at Mama's and let her see just how happy we are. Is that a plan?" I asked.

"Yes, if the trains work out," he replied. Joe took the train schedule from my hand and saw some departure times that would be convenient for us. Then he went to cancel the next day's reservation and the hotel cooperated. He paid the bill and we called my mother.

"Hi Mama, did you survive the wedding in good shape?" I asked.

"Of course, is everything alright?" she replied, a little surprised to hear from me.

"Very much so. Joe and I have run out of things to see in Milwaukee and we would like to come visit you and spend the night so we can have some time with you tomorrow. We should be there about five or so. We don't have to be back to Lawrence Hall until evening tomorrow. Now if this will be too much for you, just say so, please."

"Don't give it another thought, I'm delighted. And I will have supper ready for you."

"Thanks Mama, you are so sweet. And always remember, I love you."

"How could I forget it, when you gave me flowers on your birthday, the day you turned sixteen, to thank me for bringing you into the world. That deeply touched me and convinced me that you were entirely sincere. We will be together in a few hours, so bye for now."

We packed what little we had to pack, and I removed a green canvas shopping bag from my suitcase. Joe put our food stash in it, hoping we could eat from it on the train.

Everything went as planned and we arrived in Downers Grove about five thirty. Mama had called Arden and invited her and John to join us for dinner. They arrived at six. We were excited to see them and have a chance to learn their story. The day before, on Monday November third, John had opened his mail and received a draft notice telling him he had to report to the Army by the end of the month.

"We have chosen the twenty second of this month to get married," said Arden. "At seven thirty tonight, my parents and John's parents are going to meet with us so we can plan what's needed. The twenty second is exactly two weeks later than your date. Any tips for planning a quick wedding will be very much appreciated."

During dinner, my mother, Joe, and I shared everything we did with Arden and John, and they had some references to act on, if they chose to do so. As it turned out, only my mother and my sister Lizzie were able to attend Arden's wedding. Joe and I were not entitled to a day off for three weeks because other employees had given up their days off to cover for our honeymoon. Lizzie took notes about the wedding in shorthand and typed them out at one hundred words a minute for me to read. She had graduated from a business school before she started training to become a nurse.

Later, I did get to see the wedding of Arden's sister, Nancy, and was privileged to hear the way Arden's dad welcomed a new son-in-law into the family. He said to him, "As you leave the land of the free, you enter the home of the brave!" I've never forgotten that line.

Fifth Life
NESTING

Chapter 12

FAMILY MATTERS

———

Time seemed to be moving rapidly. Christmas was just around the corner, but I was still writing thank you notes for the wedding presents. When I finished, I turned to Christmas plans and helped the boys make paper ornaments for the tree and cards which they wanted to give to others. We had brightly colored crayons, and paper with a slight texture. We used glue to paste on fancy paper cut-outs.

We also had many different board games and kids from other dorms mixed together and got to know each other better. They developed friendships over Monopoly and card games.

New Year's Eve came and went, and we woke up in 1953. Joe returned to his college for his senior year and began his required thesis on the creation of the newest electronic device, called a transistor. He continued to be the night cook at the Hall, and I continued with my dorm mothering.

Joe and I were enjoying our life together and everything

was going as planned, until we got a phone call in mid-February. It was Dr. H calling about my mother. He said that she had the flu and was in need of care.

"Do you know anyone who might be able to stay with your mother while she recovers?" he asked. "The hospitals are so crowded they even have flu cases on beds in the hall on one floor, so I can't send her there. She does not have a severe case; her temperature is responding to the drug I gave her at the office. If she can stay in bed for a couple days and have someone who can prepare her meals and keep her resting, I can send a prescription for some vitamins and anything else she needs. I think she could be well in a week to ten days."

"I can think of one person who might be willing," I replied, "but do you have any suggestions that would keep the caretaker from being infected?"

"Yes, and if she would stop at my office, we can outfit her with a coat for isolation protection, masks, and soap to wash her hands, and gloves for whenever she touches your mother."

OK, I'll call Christine MacGarvie, she irons for Mama," I answered.

"Oh, I remember her. She was a volunteer when your Mama was involved in helping the town have a well-baby clinic for Downers Grove," Dr. H remembered. "She would be perfect. Good luck. I will call her every day and keep a close tab on your Mama. Keep in touch."

It all worked out as discussed, and Mama was ready to

return to teaching in ten days. I managed to visit her, and after talking with Mrs. MacGarvie and the other neighbor friends, I began to think that I should resign at Lawrence Hall and move in with Mama until the end of the school year.

After talking it over with Joe, he thought it would be a good idea, so next I spoke about it with Father Curzon. He listened very carefully and said, "It must be providence. Just yesterday, I had a young woman ask for an interview. She is interested in studying to possibly become a deaconess some day and wishes to find a job in a church-centered environment. She said she could be available at a moment's notice. Could you stay for two weeks and give her some orientation and training?"

"Yes," I replied. "And I hope you have as easy a time finding Joe's replacement. So, we will leave the last day of February, and be in Downers Grove on March first." We had a long talk with my mother, and she agreed to our moving in with her. She sounded relieved. I agreed to do the housework and cooking. Joe would take care of maintenance when needed, and Mama could have quiet in the evening when she needed to grade the papers she brought home. This would be easy because we had not yet bought a television set.

Joe was in luck for his long commute. The population of the western suburbs had doubled since the end of WWII. So, the Chicago, Burlington & Quincy railroad began running high-speed trains that went directly into Union Station in twenty-six minutes. These trains ran only during prime commuter time both morning and late afternoon. Once to Chicago, Joe caught the El to his school, which made his commute about an hour long.

Joe and I bought food for the household, and wanted to pay some rent to Mama for taking us in. So, I began to search for a job. I found one advertised in the local paper for the new branch location of C D Peacock in La Grange Park, Illinois, about a half hour from our house. Peacock was the first jeweler to open a store in downtown Chicago, and was the purveyor of fine jewels, china, sterling silver, and artistic decorations for the home. It was the perfect job for me! I have a passion for beautiful decor and grew up seeing precious jewels on the hands of Aunt Frances. My mind began to race. *I'm gonna love this job! I hope it pays enough to be the right job. NO, no, Edith, stop that right now. Negative thoughts are not appropriate; start picturing yourself in a store surrounded with all the beautiful things you can sell. OK, brain, I have the picture. Now I will call the store and ask for an appointment.*

The very next day I had the interview, and after checking my references, I was offered the job.

I was to be trained as the Bridal Consultant, and that required going to the main store in Chicago, where the buyer of fine china, sterling silver tableware, tea sets, platters etc. would train me. I was required to learn the names of one hundred and seven sterling place settings, fifty-six different china patterns, and know how they were manufactured, including which clay was used to make them. This took three weeks to master, and then I was sent to the La Grange store.

It was April when I started the job and I looked forward to going to work every day. Life was filled with joy. My mother thrived. Joe's research program was under way, and my sister Liz was being courted.

The fourth of July came and went. One morning, I woke up with so much nausea, I called in sick. I went back to work the next day, but I was still nauseous. Yes, I was pregnant. I had very mixed emotions about it. Part of me was delighted, and another side of me was upset because it wasn't in our plan for that year. My due date was early April of 1954.

"Stop worrying, everything is going to work out for the best," said Joe. "You know that deep in your heart you will be a terrific mother because I've seen you in action."

About six weeks later, I started to hemorrhage and lost the embryo. The loss was traumatic, in spite of making our life simpler at the time it happened. Some years when I look at a calendar and see the date that the child should have been born, I wonder if I might have had a daughter.

I continued working at Peacocks through the summer, but two weeks before the schools were to open in September, I received a call from the superintendent of the Downers Grove schools, offering me a teaching position. He had known my mother as an outstanding teacher, and she had put in a good word for me. One of their teachers had suddenly become unavailable and he thought of me. I resigned from Peacocks in good standing and they told me to contact them if I was ever available for part-time work during the Christmas season or in the summer. They said they would be glad to have me back if they needed extra help.

I signed a teacher contract to teach fifth grade at Highland School about a mile from home. We bought our first used car so I could get to my job.

When October came, my sister Liz had a lovely wedding at Grace Lutheran Church in La Grange Park. I was matron of honor and her close friends, Ruth and Betty, were bridesmaids. She was married to Gorden Cobb for forty-six years, and they had two sons and a daughter.

Joe finished his research and I typed his thesis on my little portable Underwood typewriter I bought when I started college. It was quite a responsibility, as most of the mathematical symbols were not on the keys and I had to carefully ink them into the document. Fortunately, his work was accepted, and he graduated in December. He was photographed wearing his robe and mortar board hat, making a face, and we all started laughing every time we looked at it.

A Boeing Air representative was at the college scouting graduating engineers who would move to Seattle to work on the Giant B52 Bomber. Joe was offered the job and talked it over with me and my mother. Mother was in much better health since we had moved in, and we decided that if we could find someone to do the housework, she could manage on her own.

James Straiton, a Scottish gentleman of fine character, had been renting the upstairs of the house after Liz and I no longer lived there. He and my mother had become friends, and he treated her as if she was his own "mam." He assured me and Joe that he would be home every night, and if she needed anything, he would take care of it. Now that my sister was married and had a home of her own, she could also help out.

We made a joint decision and Joe accepted the job. The only downside was that I had a contract with the Board of Education that lasted until June, and Joe would have to go to Seattle by himself. This was a plan neither of us liked, but it was necessary. Since I would have a two-week Christmas break, Joe said he wanted to go to Pennsylvania to see his parents and introduce me to them.

They welcomed me with open arms, and our short visit was interesting and fun. Stella, Joe's Mama, seemed a bit nervous as though being in a wheelchair was making her a less successful hostess. I bragged about her son, and how happy I was with him, and also how much I noticed how charming her husband was. She relaxed, and soon I was part of the family.

We stayed for three days. We had arrived by train but booked a flight to return. We took off early in the evening, when it was already dark. This was the first time I boarded an airplane, and it was a plane that held sixteen seats. About a half hour into the flight, we hit turbulence and rocked and rolled the rest of the way home.

Chapter 13

ADVANCE TO SEATTLE

———

As soon as we arrived home, it was necessary to start preparing for Joe's trip to Seattle. We had already sent a crate of household goods via railway express with an agreement it would be held until he had an address where they could deliver it. He checked into a hotel to orient himself to the city and locate the Boeing Plant.

Joe phoned to let us know that he had landed safely and said that the next thing he would look for would be a place to live. He also told me he missed me.

"Is there a possibility of finding a substitute teacher to replace you?" he asked.

"You just saw me this morning, and I miss you too, but it's hard to find a substitute teacher who agrees to work a full semester," I replied. "Just remember that I promised to love you forever, and in spite of being lonesome, this is only temporary, and you can concentrate on learning your new job. My heart is with you my darling. It went with you today, but it's bedtime here in Illinois. So take my heart with you. Then let's say good night, ok? I love you and hope you sleep well, and may God bless you Joseph. Good night my love." It was difficult to hang up, but we did it together.

The following day I was back with my overcrowded fifth grade class, and I discovered that ten-year-old kids were a special age group, and I really appreciated them. Their lives are about to change. They are at the threshold of becoming more rational beings, but still maintain some characteristics of a young child. The dichotomy made it important to choose my words carefully at times.

One day, while I was writing some new words on the board, two boys started whispering to each other. I turned to face them.

"You know better than to start a conversation during a lesson," I said. "Should you or anyone else do so, you will serve time after school. Is that perfectly clear?"

Another boy named Jackson, who sat next to the whisperer, raised his hand up.

"That's not fair," he chimed in. "I didn't get to hear the answer Jim gave Tom, so I don't know what happened."

"This has nothing to do with fairness. The issue is paying attention to the lesson you are working on," I explained. "You can ask Jim what he said after school. Now look at the blackboard and tell me what the first word is."

"I don't know," said Jackson.

"That's the reason I'm presenting these words," I answered. "Instead of having the whole class look them up, you are learning them before you read the story. Tomorrow we are going to read a very exciting story about a famous detective in London, England named Sherlock Holmes. The name of the story is *The Hound of the Baskervilles*."

I told them more about the story and then we practiced saying the words and their meanings. This project took several days, and the story had so much wicked suspense, the kids were waiting eagerly for the next installment.

Every day after school, the first thing I did was look for the mail. Joe wrote to me almost every day. He kept repeating over and over how much he loved me, and that he was so bored that he went to bed as early as seven or eight in the evening. In his next letter, he said he had a tooth that was bothering him and he went to a dentist who cleaned just the one tooth and filled it for fifteen dollars. Compared to Chicago area prices, this was such a bargain that the next day he had all his teeth cleaned, and a molar extracted. The total bill was less than seventy dollars. His next comment was in "engineer speak." He wrote, I love you, I miss you, I love you, $x10^{27}$. I wondered why he chose twenty-seven for the strength of the power and remembered that twenty-seven is the day of my birthday. I was thrilled by the magnitude of the equation, and appreciated, once again, how clever Joe was.

Back at Highland School, the Sherlock Holmes project was coming to an end, and the kids enjoyed their first taste of classic literature. Some of the most advanced readers went to the library and checked out additional books about Sherlock Holmes. Some said their parents told them that they had also read those books when they were in school. Expanded reading had hooked several students, who then set new learning skills for themselves. I was happy they were happy. Growth was occurring both physically and intellectually.

Early in February, a new student joined our class. His name was Jonas and he was a refugee child from Yugoslavia. Jonas wore a small mesh bag filled with garlic and herbs around his neck to keep evil spirits away, and we had a round of coughing from some of the students and some holding of noses. *Dear God, how do I handle this?* I thought. Fortunately, I didn't have to worry about it.

The school nurse walked in the door and said she needed to check Jonas' scalp because she had just examined his third-grade sister and found that she had a head covered with lice. As she was combing through his hair with her fingers and peering over every inch, a first-grade child came into the room with a note for me from the principal. He stared at the nurse with her hands in Jonas' hair, looking carefully through each strand, and innocently asked, "Did you lose something?" The whole room erupted in laughter. Then she asked Jonas to come with her and they left the room. She returned a few minutes later to explain what had happened, told the children about lice, and said that anyone who felt like they might have them needed to tell me. I would let the nurse know.

"Right now we are printing a letter that you can take home with you to inform your parents about the lice, and that it is easy to get rid of them if you follow directions, or consult your doctor," the nurse said.

Just like that, my problem with Jonas disappeared. He was transferred to another school where they worked with children who did not speak English.

January was passing rapidly, and Joe's letters indicated he was occupied with evaluating different housing projects and neighborhoods. He wanted to find something suitable for the two of us.

The principal of my school was Mr. Collet, and he was also the principal of Mama's school. They were old friends. When Mr. Collet was told about my marriage, he told my mother that he would keep watching to see if there were any new applicants or anyone interviewing who might be able to replace me. He told Mama that long separations were sometimes bad for a marriage, and he didn't want that to happen to me.

As luck would have it, a teaching candidate applied in early February. His name was Dick Whitlock and Dick and I were in the same class in school. In the winter, the police would cordon off Bryan Place, the street I lived on. It was on a hill, so the kids could sled down it during a certain time of day. All the neighbors agreed to do it for years. Dick would come over and join me in sledding. Later, he attended the University of Utah on probation because of his academic record. He did well there and not only finished his degree but completed a Ph.D. at the University of California in San Jose. Now, he agreed to take over the class the first of March. Yippee!

I was so excited I could hardly wait to call Joe when I got home, but Seattle time is two hours behind us, so I had to wait. In the meantime, Mama came home and was very happy for me.

I called at eight-thirty that evening, and when I gave him the news, he was speechless for several seconds. "You really can come? In four weeks? I'm so happy I can hardly speak," he said. Then we went on to talk for about ten minutes. We made plans and determined our separate responsibilities for making the move go smoothly.

Meanwhile, Joe found us a place to live. It was a basement apartment in a home in west Seattle overlooking Puget Sound. The house was high on a hill and to reach the front door you had to mount a stairway composed of both steps and zigzag ramps. If it had nothing but steps, it would have had twenty-seven steps. The entire stairway was made of rock, and one of the ramps had a large rock that was very smooth which jutted out to form a seat to rest on before you climbed the next group of stairs. When you arrived at the top and turned around to face the ocean on a clear day, you could see the majesty of the Olympic Mountains.

Joe was very busy and moved in a week before I arrived. The apartment consisted of one large room with a sofa bed for sleeping, a closet, a narrow bathroom with a shower, and a nice kitchen with a stove, refrigerator, and a table with four chairs. The place was basically unfurnished. He called railway express and they delivered our household possessions. Then he had a telephone installed and went to Sears and bought a small dresser.

My plane landed on time and Joe came running toward me and gave me a kiss and a most enjoyable hug. Holding hands, we went to the luggage pickup and while we waited, Joe asked me, "Are you hungry?"

"Only for you," I answered, watching a broad grin appear very quickly on his face.

"Are you sure you don't want to go out to dinner? I did get some food in the apartment, but you look so good in your new suit you don't look like you belong at a kitchen table," he said.

"I just want to be with you," I explained. "I'm not ready to be surrounded by people I don't know."

"Great, just what I hoped. Hey, isn't that your luggage?" he asked, pointing to the carousel.

We grabbed my bags and loaded them on a cart. Then we went out to see if any of the buses that brought Joe to the airport were still in the area. Luck was with us and soon we were en route to our new home.   When several passengers left the bus, Joe walked up to speak to the driver. He came back and said, "We're almost there, but you will get your first look through the window because we are going past it. LOOK out right now, to the top of the hill." Then the bus slowed and stopped at a corner, just a short distance up the road. Joe took the suitcase, and I had the carry-on when we exited. I was a bit confused, but I figured Joe was up to something, and I'd soon find out. He put the suitcase on the sidewalk, took my hand, and walked me back toward the house. We stopped in front of the zig-zag steps.

"We live in the back side of the house, so you won't need to climb these unless you want the exercise," he told me. Then he turned us around and picked up the suitcase and we went up the street that was less steep. The driveway to our place was right there.

We entered the back door to the apartment, leaving the luggage on the ground, and Joe acted as tour guide. We walked down the hall and Joe pointed out the bathroom door and then opened the door to the heart of our home. The kitchen was full of light from the window overlooking the garden. He had set the table with a nice tablecloth and had two place settings of our silverware, and our wedding dishes on the table. On the center of the table was a vase with a dozen red roses. He certainly had planned a most gracious welcome, and I instantly felt I was home.

Chapter 14

FRIENDS AND VISITORS

———

Being together again was a great blessing to both of us. We went shopping for a comfortable chair, an end table, and a lamp to make our main room more livable. The Barton family, who lived upstairs, were very nice people and treated us like friends. They were a middle-aged couple and a very close family. They had an adopted 13-year-old daughter named Jeannette and were very close friends with her biological mother and father. Jeannette's mother had died when Jeannette was only an infant so Mrs. Barton cared for her for a year before asking the father if he would sign over parental rights to her. Jeannette called her father "uncle." She was always allowed to know her birth family and had a loving connection with them. Mrs. Barton also adopted a little baby boy a few years later, and then she got pregnant and gave birth to two more boys, Charlie and Byron. She was also the caretaker of a little girl whose mother worked full time. She brought them over at seven in the morning and picked her up at 5:30 in the evening. A house of kids. Lots of fun.

On weekends, we went sightseeing. Toward the end of April, we caught a ferry and traveled to Victoria, British Columbia, the city of the Provincial Parliament. Our first view of Victoria was from the ferry looking toward the Empress Hotel and government buildings. The streets were decorated with enormous hanging baskets of flowers. It is a city of gardens, and we caught a tour bus to the world famous Butchart Gardens. The views were so astonishing and spectacular that I felt like I was reading the mind of God when He was thinking about creating beauty in the world.

Joe appreciated it all, as I did, but it also had another dimension that thrilled him--the engineering. The gardens were built inside an abandoned quarry from the family's cement business. They were left with a fifty-acre hole in the ground. Mrs. Butchart asked her husband if they could turn it into a beautiful garden. They hired engineers, soil experts, etc., but Mrs. Butchart was the steam behind the project, which took four years to build. The garden included roads, fountains, woods, ethnic themes, large flat areas, rolling hills, and bridges. Joe was so impressed that he bought a booklet about the engineering challenges.

After strolling around the breathtaking gardens, we went to the tea house where we had high tea. We enjoyed sitting down and resting our feet. While relaxing, Joe asked me, "Would you like to make plans for next week?"

"What do you have in mind?" I asked.

"I saw an ad in the paper that might be of interest to you. It was an ad about the opening of a broadway play called *The King and I*. Would you like me to get tickets?"

"Oh, it would be wonderful to see a live production. Yes, buy the tickets. Please."

We were able to see the show and it was the only time we ever saw Yul Brenner in person. He had an excellent interpretation of the King.

Joe developed a friendship with another Boeing engineer who started in the required class the same day he did, so we were beginning to have a social life. His friend was known by his initials, which were SM. SM and his wife Beverly came for dinner a couple of times, but if we asked them to do something with us on the weekend, they weren't available. They were of the Mormon faith and the church sponsored a community garden for their members, who pledged hours of time to work in the garden. They either froze or canned their share so they would always have a supply of food. Judy Richardson, a close friend and sorority sister from Northwestern, was teaching in Tacoma. She came for a visit one Saturday, and we had a nice reunion.

The next visitor was a surprise. My mother called and said she would like to come to Seattle for a visit.

"What a great idea," I said, "but there is one problem. I'll have to figure out where you can sleep."

"Oh, that's not a big problem," she replied. "I have a cousin in Seattle, and I called her and told her that I was coming to visit you and she said stay a day or two with us.... so I took her up on it. She said they would pick me up at the airport when my plane arrives on Saturday and when I wanted to go to your place, they would drive me, if that's alright with you."

"That's good planning. You get two visits done with one trip. When will you be here?"

"The second Saturday in June," Mama answered. "I will call you after I land and let you know I made it. And then I'll see you on Tuesday morning."

"This is really wonderful," I replied. "Joe will probably be as excited as I am. He misses you too. You're one of his favorite people."

"Then give him a kiss for me. And I will see you soon. Goodbye," she finished, and we hung up.

I told Mrs. Barton that Mama was coming for a visit.

"You two haven't bought an extra bed, have you?" she asked.

"Not yet, but we're trying to find a good solution."

"Well, you can relax. Our daughter is going to be visiting with some relatives," she said. "Just what week will your mom be here?"

I told Mrs. Barton of Mama's plan to stay with her cousin who would bring her to our house on Tuesday.

"Perfect," she replied. "That's during the time Jeanette should be gone and I'm sure she won't mind letting your Mama use her room."

Ten minutes later, Jeanette came downstairs and knocked on our kitchen door. She told me she would be glad to share her space and she hoped that she might get back early enough to meet Mama because the flight to Chicago didn't leave until late afternoon. What a sweet girl!

While we were having dinner, I told Joe about Mama's call. His eyes lit up and a big smile appeared when he said, "I need to go to the hardware store and get something to tighten the window. Ever since the earthquake, it rattles if it gets windy. Want to come with me?"

That earthquake had occurred about a week earlier. We had gone to bed and when we woke up, one of the doors of our kitchen cabinets was open. Some of our coffee cups had fallen out into the sink and several of their handles had broken off. We saw no other damage inside or outside the apartment, except for the window, which still rattled in the wind. When we turned on the radio that day, we were amazed we had slept through an earthquake! Now, Joe was right, it was a good time to fix the window.

"Are you sure you should fix it?" I asked. "Perhaps we should tell Mr. Barton."

"They won't care if I do it. It's only going to take a few minutes," he replied. "I looked it over last night, so I know what I need. I repeat, would you like to give me the pleasure of your company?"

"Not right now," I replied, thinking ahead. "As you know, the window is over the sink, and the dishes need to be washed and the counter needs to be cleaned. This will give you room to work. We don't need any more broken cups and the quake sure did enough damage to that wall."

"You're right. It's a good thing I married a smart woman," he teased. "Since you aren't coming, how about a goodbye kiss?"

"I won't resist," I replied, sidling up to him and kissing him. "Wow! I'll see you later. Bye."

He returned home much later than expected, loaded down with so many packages I couldn't imagine how he had managed them all on the bus.

"It looks like you went someplace other than the hardware store," I observed.

"I bumped into SM at the mall and he offered me a ride home. While I'm unwrapping this stuff, would you do me a favor and sit down in the kitchen with your eyes shut? Don't open them until I tell you."

I did what he asked, and as I sat there with my eyes shut, I could hear him moving around the room humming a happy song. He seemed to be very happy, or perhaps even excited.

"Hey, Red," he said, using his nickname for me from his letters, "You can open your eyes now, and step into my parlor."

I did and was astonished by the improvement he had made in the room. On each end of the sofa were bright-colored, plumped pillows. He had placed a rug with similar colors to the pillows in front of the sofa, and he opened two boxes which contained two small tables that needed assembly. The formerly dull room was now bright and colorful.

"If you don't like it, it can all be returned," he said.

"No way, I love it, but what motivated you tonight?"

"Thinking about your mother coming. You earned this," he explained. "When Mrs. B went to Missouri to care for her sick mother for a month, you earned enough extra money taking care of Susie, Mrs. B's day care kid."

"Well, it certainly looks a lot more "homey." Thanks, you did a beautiful job," I said, truly touched by his thoughtfulness and interior design sense. "It's gotten so late now; why don't you fix the window in the morning when you can see better? Let's go to bed now."

Before we knew it, the second Saturday of June arrived. Mama called from her cousin's home and told us that they were going to take her to Butchart Garden on Sunday, because no one should miss seeing it. They could rent a special wheelchair at the Gardens that was designed for comfort even on long, long walks. They would take the car on the ferry and have it for getting around the island. I could see that they were used to planning for the elderly, and Mama's cousin Helen was a high-energy, very gracious lady with graying hair, who was close to my mother's age.

Tuesday morning, I put a tablecloth on the table and set it with some fresh flowers from the back garden, and some caramel pecan rolls I baked the day before, along with a bowl of fresh berries and everything else needed for tea. I called Helen and told her to come up the side street to avoid the stairs, and to park in the driveway close to the garage. Then I went out back and waited for their arrival.

It was a great reunion, with hugs and kisses before we entered the house. It was great to meet Helen in person after talking to her on the phone. She was a very charming, gracious woman from my German grandmother's side of the family. I had them sit on the sofa or the other chair in the room and said, "Except for the bathroom, you have seen it all!" They both laughed and shared what their lives were like when they were first married.

At noon, we moved to the kitchen table and I put the kettle on. I offered to make sandwiches, but they were in favor of having more than one caramel pecan roll. I called Mrs. B and asked her if she would like to join us. I had made so many rolls that I gave her a half dozen to take home for her kids. She came and stayed about twenty minutes, then went upstairs to see to the children, who were already napping.

When Joe got home, he went straight to my mother and gave her a real bear hug.

"Howdy stranger, welcome to Seattle," he said. Then he introduced himself to Helen, and they conversed while I was preparing dinner. For meat, we had a Seattle specialty--a chicken pheasant, which is a delicious cross between those two birds, developed by a local farmer.

Helen left after dinner, and Mrs. B suggested that Mama might like to come up and see her   bedroom. Joe picked up her suitcase and carried it upstairs for her. Then Mr. Barton asked if we would like to see a movie which was starting at eight o'clock. Mama accepted, and we all watched it together.

The week passed rapidly and we just stayed home and enjoyed being together. We did take Mama out to dinner on Thursday night. The restaurant was close enough to walk to except the hills were too steep for Mama, so we called a cab to take us there and bring us home.

Friday was our last evening with her and she told us all the Downers Grove news she had been keeping to herself. First, she told us that Mr. Straiton had married a lovely Canadian woman from Winnipeg and was now teaching his parakeet to speak the sentence, "Take me to Winnipeg," with his Scottish accent. He moved out but told Mama that his oldest friend from childhood was coming to live in Downers and would need a place for his family until they could find a permanent place to live. This would keep the house occupied while she was in Seattle. It was the typical way Scots take care of their friends, and Mama thought it a good idea.

Joe always liked our cat, Nutmeg, and he asked about him. Mama told Joe that Nutmeg had disappeared many months ago, and they searched for him. She had even called the police to ask if anyone had reported a stray cat, or if anyone had hit one with their car.

"Do you remember that he had a funny dark mark on his nose?" Mama asked Joe.

Joe shook his head no.

"A few weeks ago, I went over to the Cloverleaf Dairy on Forest Avenue. I looked onto the side yard of the house and there were multiple cats with food and water bowls. Right in the middle of a harem, Nutmeg had found himself a new home. Smart cat!"

Helen came over about one o'clock to take us all to the airport. We sat with Mama in the terminal until they announced her call to board the plane. She was wheeled onto the plane and seated early.

We watched the plane take off and wondered when we would see her again.

Chapter 15

A New Horizon

———

Shortly after my mother left, both Joe and I seemed to be rather restless. Her visit with us had strengthened our bond with her. We found our conversations filled with memories of the time we lived with her. Joe shared his feelings when he said, "I never knew that a mother-in- law could be so funny or so precious." It was such a gracious compliment. Tears came to my eyes, and I marveled at Joe's capacity to love.

When he saw me wipe the tears away, he took my hand and pulled me closer to him while we were sitting on the sofa, and gently, just above a whisper he said, "We need to talk." He put his arm around my shoulder.

"Edie, I've been doing a lot of thinking lately," he began, "and I think I want to make a change. I've been considering what kind of a future I have at Boeing and what chance there is for promotion. If anything should go wrong with Boeing, and there was a layoff, Seattle is not a city that has much for my type of engineering other than at Boeing.

"I have been doing research about the job market and where it would probably be best for us to live, and at the present time it seems to be the Midwest, and the Chicago area. This is the year your Mama is going to turn seventy, and she told us it's her last year they will allow her to teach. I know you like this climate, but would you consider moving back to Downers Grove, where we can keep an eye on your mother?"

I was startled. "When you said you were thinking about change, you weren't kidding."

"True, and I don't want to rush you," Joe replied. "I'd like you to sleep on it and take a day or two to decide. However, if you are in favor of making the move, keep in mind that it is already mid- July, and we will have a lot to do. I have to find the best time to resign and give them time to give me a recommendation."

"Well, Joseph, I already know the answer," I said. "If you can work all this out to your satisfaction, we leave. In the morning, I'll start packing; do you want to fly or should we rent a car to drive? I'm guessing that a car rental and gasoline would be much cheaper than two plane tickets, and we might be able to take more of our stuff with us."

"Amazing!" said Joseph. "You're already a step ahead of me."

"So why don't I call the rental car dealerships and get prices for different cars, the price of gasoline, and if they have an agency in the Chicago area to return the car there,"

I said. "Then, I'll look up motel chains and ask them to mail us brochures so we can plan possible stops for the nights we drive. Can you think of anything else?"

"Yeah, let's get off this sofa, open it up, and turn it into our bed," said Joe. "Care to join me?"

"Silly!" is all I said.

* * * * *

Once again, good fortune came our way. Joe sat down at a lunch table with another engineer named Fred. They started chatting and discovered they were both thinking of resigning. They kept their voices low as they schemed.

"Why don't you meet me in the parking lot after work?" said Fred. "I'm going to Chicago and driving my own car. If we could share the cost of the gas, we would both save money. Interested?"

Joe shook his head yes, and Fred handed him a slip of paper with his parking area number.

When they met, they asked each other personal questions about why they were dissatisfied, why they wanted to go to the Midwest and what the consequences would be for their family. They exchanged business cards and Joe discovered Fred was an engineer of a higher rank. That spoke for both his intelligence and integrity, so Joe asked him if he'd like to come to dinner.

Fred asked Joe where his car was parked, and Joe told

him that he took the bus to work. "Well," said Fred, "I will drive you home. If we are going to spend three or four days together in a car, it will give you a chance to see if you think you want to make the deal. They exchanged their home phone numbers.

Joe walked in the door with a jaunty step, and a happy smile. He swooped me up and twirled me around in a joyous, swinging hug and said, "Have I got a story for you!"

He proceeded to tell me all the details of his experience meeting Fred, and how Fred offered him a ride home. "I'd like to phone him tonight and invite him to dinner tomorrow. Is that okay with you?"

"Sure, but let's figure out what you want me to cook, so I can go to the store if I need anything."

Joe took a minute to think. "Make something simple, like spaghetti, meatballs, and a salad, garlic bread, and ice cream for dessert. I think you can get most of that ready-made."

"Right now, let's eat what I fixed for tonight," I said. "Then call him about tomorrow."

Fred accepted our invitation, and I told Joe that at twenty-seven cents a gallon, multiplied by two thousand miles, gasoline would cost approximately five hundred and forty dollars, give or take a few dollars. A solid estimate would be six hundred dollars, so divided in two, our half of the trip would be three hundred. Add three or four motels at forty dollars a night and that would run one hundred and sixty dollars. My hope was to shorten one of the driving days so we could stop and visit Yellowstone National Park.

The next day we had an enjoyable dinner with Fred and he said that a stop at Yellowstone was possible if we would limit it to no more than two hours. He apologized for being in such a hurry, and then explained he was worried about his wife. She was in her fourth month of pregnancy and her doctor had suggested she stay with her mother because she was suffering from pernicious nausea and needed to be on bed rest until it subsided. The doctor gave her the name of another physician who was in medical school with him and arranged for him to oversee the case while she was in Illinois.

"She's doing much better, but I can't just let her go through all this alone," Fred said. "That's my child and we both want him or her to live."

Fred excused himself because he wanted to call her and tell her he would be with her on September seventh. Actually, the real date was the fifth, but he added the two days so if we encountered detours or road repair zones, she wouldn't worry if we were delayed.

We spent the rest of the month packing and saying goodbyes to our few friends.

On September first, at six-thirty in the morning, we loaded our stuff into Fred's car and headed for Spokane. Joe sat in the front seat with Fred as the driver. Sitting in the back gave me a good vantage point to watch the beautiful mountains. Fred had a new Buick and it was quite comfortable and roomy.

After lunch and a pit stop, we started to drive faster. We were singing *Go Tell It On The Mountain*, followed by *He's Got the Whole World in His Hands*. Fred and I were the singers; Joe didn't know those old folk classics. A few minutes later, while peering out the window, I began to feel nauseated. Oh NO. I'm not going to be nauseated. NO NO. As a child I would often get carsick, and I didn't want it to come back. Fortunately, I had brought my favorite pillow along, and I told the guys I was tired and falling asleep. I put the pillow down, stretched out on the back seat and slept soundly until the next stop. I was just fine.

When we reached the highest altitude the next day, again I didn't feel like eating anything, and nausea struck again. I remembered what happened when we went over the divide when I was on my way to camp and joined in the fun of the trip. Once I was on flat land again, I was fine. I turned on my biggest smile, and acted like I knew how to talk, and we found a few songs Joe knew too. We amused ourselves from the tedium by making complete fools of ourselves. We restrained ourselves from singing *Ninety-Nine Bottles of Beer On The Wall*, and all was forgiven.

We pulled into Bryan Place in Downers Grove, and Mama was just coming home from teaching, looking tired. She seemed astounded to see us but gave us a lovely welcome. It was good to be back, but I couldn't help wondering what was next.

Chapter 16

LUCKY BREAKS

———

We arrived in Downers Grove two days after Labor Day, around two o'clock in the afternoon. It was a day earlier than Mama had expected us. We were excited, but our excitement faded a little when we realized that she was still at school, because classes had already started.

We unloaded our stuff from Fred's car, placing it on the grass of the front yard. We were all hungry, so I said I'd go into the kitchen to see if there was any food to make sandwiches and something to drink. There was a good supply and Fred, Joe, and I sat down at the table with some apple juice and sandwiches. Then we paid Fred for our share of the fuel, thanked him for the trip, and exchanged phone numbers as we said goodbye.

As soon as he left, we went upstairs to see if there were any Scottish people living there. The whole house was immaculate, and Phemee had left a note on one of the beds which said:

Dear Edith,

Welcome home. Your mother was so gracious to us, and as she refused to accept any money, Harry and I took it upon ourselves to do a thorough cleaning, both up and down. I hope you find it to your liking. We hope to meet you soon.

Phemee

I was glad she spelled her nickname so I could pronounce it when we met, because I knew it was the intimate, personal version of the Gaelic name, Euphemia.

Joe and I went outside and began bringing our things into the house and cluttering up the living room. When we were almost finished, Mama appeared, walking down the sidewalk, looking tired. When she focused on us, her face lit up with a joyful smile, and she hurried to hug us both. Mama and I went inside and sat together on the sofa.

"Do you have a good class this year?" I asked her.

"Yes. I have a special class this year," she replied. "The principal, Mr. Colett usually assigns the difficult kids to me, because he knows that I am very good at working with kids who see themselves as losers. However, this year he gave me a group of bright kids and told me to enjoy the year."

"How wonderful! I'm so happy for you, Mama," I replied happily. "You spent so many years helping the poor readers! I'm also glad you're teaching third grade now and on the first floor, so you don't have to climb the stairs anymore.

"I doubt that you remember it, but one day I came home early from school to let you know I had an extra rehearsal that day at four o'clock in addition to the one already scheduled at seven o'clock that evening. Since I knew that I'd be on the train to La Grange when you finished work and nowhere near a telephone, I decided to walk over and tell you about the change in schedule. I had a note ready, in case you were busy, and you were. You and some other teachers were in the breakroom at lunchtime and I heard one say to you, 'Esther, you're wasting your time staying after school with that Polish kid. Don't you know he has a low IQ and doesn't have much to give?' Then I heard you answer, 'Well, that may have been true last year when you had him, but I'm counting on his IQ being several points higher by the end of this year!' I was so proud of you, and now you have time for some fun. You've earned it!"

Joe entered the room. "I never heard that story about you, but I just discovered that I never want to say the wrong thing to you because you'll have the perfect put down," he joked. Mama just started laughing and muttered something about Joe having excellent hearing.

We were all tired and hungry, so Joe grabbed the phonebook and looked for the name of a restaurant. He asked if the Last Word on Ogden was any good, and we said yes. He called for a taxi.

While at dinner, we discussed our priorities. The first thing we needed to do, of course, was to find Joe a job.

"I would like to take a couple of days to get organized, and see what would work for me," I said. I wanted to see the neighbors alone and get a truthful report on Mama and how she had been doing. In the morning after Mama left, I went outside and sat on the steps of the small front porch. I noticed that the two flower beds on either side of the steps were full of weeds and had no flowers in them. I remembered that it used to be my job to plant annuals every spring. I was beginning to pull the weeds, when I thought I heard someone say my name. I turned around and saw Mrs. Johnson, who lived at the top of Bryan Hill, standing there on the sidewalk. I used to babysit for her when I was in my teens.

"Edith, are you here for a visit?" she asked.

"No, Joe decided he could find better engineering opportunities in this area," I explained. "He had a good recommendation from Boeing and we both thought my mother needed us to be here, so we took a giant leap of faith and came back."

"Good. I wish you all the best," she replied, brightly. "But I better finish my walk and let you finish your gardening. Bye for now!" And she left.

The day went by quickly, and after supper, the doorbell rang. I went to answer it and was very surprised to see Mr. Johnson, the husband of the lady who had stopped to talk with me in the morning.

"I came to meet your husband," he said. "I need some

help, and my wife Elizabeth says that Dorothy Cowart told her that he was a great handyman who could fix most anything."

"Just a minute," I replied. "He's in the basement. I'll call him. Do come in, Mr. Johnson." Mr. Johnson stepped into the living room while I went to the top of the basement stairs.

"Joe, one of our neighbors, Mr. Johnson is here and would like to meet you!" I called.

Joe came right up and gave me a look of confusion that asked what the devil was going on. We entered the living room and I made the introductions.

"I am involved in a neighborhood project, and I could use an assistant," began Mr. Johnson. "Across the street, three houses up the hill, there lives a widow who is aging rapidly and her front steps into the house have no railings for her to hold onto. She's hard to get along with and all the kids hate her because she yells at them when they are playing outside. But most of us show her respect, even if she doesn't return it. I'm buying two iron railings and will install them, but I could use a hand to steady them while I work. Would you be willing to do that with me?"

"Sure, be glad to help," replied Joe.

"Well, having roped you in, I'd also like to know a little more about you. Tell me about yourself."

"Well, we just moved back here from Seattle, and at the moment I am an unemployed engineer with a good recommendation from Boeing," explained Joe.

"Are you an aeronautical engineer?" Mr. Johnson asked.

"No, I'm an electrical engineer and I've worked with radar and some of the new electronic equipment."

"This is almost unbelievable, Joe. I am in electrical too. I've been employed with Western Electric for several years. Right now, we are looking for young engineers who would like to build a career with us. If you are interested, I'd be willing to set up an interview for you. I can send you some literature about the company and some information about what we are looking for in an interview. How does that sound?"

Joe was stunned but elated when he replied, "It sounds like answer to a prayer. Thank you so much."

"I will let you have the rest of your evening," Mr. Johnson said. "I will keep in touch about the project. Here's one of my business cards. I hope I'll see you within the week. Goodnight."

Joe and I looked at each other. Fate was on our side again.

* * * * *

The next morning, Joe put our trip clothes into the washing machine and hung them on the line in the backyard. He wanted to make sure that his clothes were nice and clean in case Mr. Johnson called about the interview. Between the military and helping me at Lawrence Hall, Joe was a laundry expert.

Helen, from across the street, came over to see me. She told me that she thought my mother was very lonesome and had slowed down in general, even though her motto was still, "I'm going to live until I die with my boots on!" Helen feared her health was going downhill and told me she hoped Joe and I could move in with her. On her lunch hour from work, Dorothy from next door took the time to come and see me and tell me the same thing. That settled it. There was no other choice and Joe agreed with me. When Mama came home from school, we would tell her we wanted to stay right where we were and make our home with her.

When we gave her the news, Mama formed a smile that stretched across her face from ear to ear, and her eyes sparkled like two sapphires in sunlight. She radiated joy and took my hand in hers. "I've been hoping you would say that; in fact, I wanted to tell you that it was my prayer, but I didn't want to get in the way if you had other plans," she said happily. She let go of my hand, turned to Joe, and gave him a quick kiss on the cheek.

We were just sitting down together when the phone rang. It was Mr. Johnson calling Joe.

Joe took the phone and acknowledged that he was listening. A couple of minutes passed and finally, we heard Joe reply. "Okay, I'll be there. Thank you. Goodbye."

We turned toward Joe, looking him straight in the eye with a question mark written on their faces. Mr. Johnson was either calling about the railing or the interview. Joe sat down with us again.

"I got the appointment at Western Electric," he said happily. "The interview is at three o'clock tomorrow afternoon, and Mr. Johnson says I can ride home with him. If all goes well, and I get this job, Edie, we may even be able to buy that car we've been talking about!"

"That would be wonderful," I replied happily. "I'm tired of depending on trains."

We were all very happy and filled with hope. Joe went off to iron his shirt and make sure that his suit and tie were in good shape for the interview.

Then the phone rang again. It was my sister, Lizzie. I told her we were living with Mama.

"Oh Edith, that's such good news."

We finished our dinner happily, looking forward to the future.

Sixth Life
MOTHERHOOD

Chapter 17

THORNS AND ROSES

———

While Joe was getting everything ready for his interview the following day, I locked myself in the bathroom to read a letter. It wasn't exactly bad news. My doctor in Seattle suggested that I see Dr. W soon. The letter contained test reports and some results were borderline normal, which meant something was just a little out of sync, but treatable. Alleluia! So I tucked the letter back into my pocket, went to the room where the telephone was located, and called for an appointment.

The receptionist said that Dr. W had received a letter from Seattle and was expecting me to call. I told her that I needed an appointment time that would coincide with the train schedule as I did not have a car. She said their office was a block north of the tracks, gave me directions, and told me they had a cancellation for the next day at three o'clock in the afternoon. Perfect, I thought. Joe would be at his interview and rush hour trains stopped at LaGrange, so I figured I'd get home before he would.

At my appointment, Dr. W told me I was pregnant. I was delighted! He then gave me a prescription for a new drug that helped women who had previously miscarried to carry to term and have a normal delivery. I left feeling very pleased and hopeful that all would be well.

As I sat on the train going home, I got to thinking about all the babies that I would be meeting soon. Arden and John were back in Downers, as he had been discharged from the army and Arden was due in April. My sister was due in December, and if all went well for me, April or early May would be my due date.

I was walking home from the train station when I saw Mr. Johnson drop Joe off at the house. I was on Bryan Place in the lower block and the house we lived in was a block ahead, up a steep hill, offering a clear view of the lower block. Joe saw me and started running toward me. When we met face to face, he grabbed my hand with great excitement.

"I start on Monday!" he said joyfully. Then he hugged and kissed me, right there on the sidewalk in front of all the neighbors. He talked about his interview nonstop, all the way home, and kept on talking so Mama could hear all about it. Mama. That's what I called my mother because that was her name all my life. Suddenly, I wondered what my own child would call me.

Mama was so sure that Joe would return home employed that she had decided to cook a real celebration dinner. I set the table with our best china and some wine glasses. Joe was honored. He poured the wine and when he got to my glass, I put my hand over the top of it and said, "No thanks, I want ginger ale."

"What do you mean? You're not going to drink to me?" he teased with a playful expression.

"No, I don't mean that at all. I just don't want any alcohol," I replied, automatically, like a typical pregnant woman.

"Since when?" Joe pressed me.

I decided to come clean. "Since three-thirty this afternoon when the doctor told me I'm pregnant," I answered, without thinking. Then suddenly, I realized what I had said. "Oh my God," I blurted out, raising my right hand to cover my mouth.

My mother looked delighted, but Joe looked like he might be in a state of shock. I just sat there quietly, holding my breath, until he could reply. Mama sensed the tension.

"Excuse me, you two need to be alone," said my mother, and she picked up her plate and went to eat in the kitchen.

"How come I didn't know anything about this?" he asked in a calm, thoughtful voice.

I let out the deep breath I'd been holding as I waited for Joe's response. "I'm so sorry...I didn't mean to take you by surprise. And I didn't want you to worry about it. After all, I have already lost a baby twice and was hoping that I could find out if the medical profession had some help for me," I told him. "However, there is a temporary restriction. Sexual contact is to be limited to cuddling, and kissing, and nothing more until we pass the third month, because that's when I lost the other two. But that's only three weeks away."

"So you've seen the doctor already. Does he have any hours on Saturday, or in the evening? I want to meet him and learn what my part is in keeping you well."

"Yes. He gave me his office hours," I said. "He did warn me that sometimes he has to cancel appointments because babies often come at inconvenient times, but his nurse always calls to immediately reschedule the appointment."

I called my mother back into the dining room. "Mama, we need to go back to celebrating Joe's new job," I said. "Did you make any dessert? Let's have it now and tell him how wonderful he is." That's just what we did. We found even more to talk about, and we just enjoyed being together.

When Sunday came, Mama was the only woman in the room who wasn't pregnant. My sister and Gordon had joined us, and we invited Arden and John. As often occurs at social gatherings, the men got together to talk about their army experiences and cars. We women were more inclined to talk about babies. However, this time when the talk turned to automobiles amongst the guys, I perked up my ears and asked for opinions about the most trustworthy dealer in the area. John said his father trusted the Ford dealer because he didn't have a large lot of used cars. The few he had were reconditioned trade-ins that even had limited warranties.

A few days later, John's suggestion paid off. We bought

our first car--a small, light green Plymouth. At the end of October, we took a long drive north and dropped Mama off at my sister's house for a visit. Then, as we were so near the Wisconsin border, we continued north to enjoy the abundance of the fall colors. I was surprised by Joe's reaction to the flatness of the land we were traversing.

"Where are the hills?" he asked. It had never occurred to me that he had never lived anywhere without mountains except Illinois. I told him that as we traveled further north into Wisconsin that he would encounter hills the size of foothills for larger mountains, but most of the Midwest was flat for hundreds of miles.

On the way home, I began to have light abdominal cramps. When they started to get stronger, we were near Des Plaines and Joe stopped the car at a public phone and called the doctor. Dr. W told him to hurry to the hospital in Hinsdale and asked for the number on our license plate. Apparently, he shared it with the state police, along with the route we were driving because about five minutes later, a state police car pulled up beside Joe's window. The trooper inside motioned to Joe to follow him, increased his car's speed, and turned on the flashing lights. As a caravan, we accelerated to eighty-five miles per hour on a two-lane highway. It was so frightening it took my mind off my pain completely.

Unsurprisingly, we arrived at the hospital very quickly. It was strange that one of my first thoughts was that I was happy we had made it there before my bleeding messed up our new car. Eventually, we found out that for some unknown reason, my body did not react to the drug properly. We were both once more disappointed and distressed. This failure made it three heartbreaks too many.

I was in the hospital for a day and a half before the doctor came to tell me I could go home and I should get some extra sleep and take it easy for a week. Then he offered me some hope by telling me that in a few weeks, if my cycle returned and seemed normal, he could perform a simple operation called a "D&C," which I had never heard of before. It meant Dilation and Curettage and was a common procedure to clear the uterine lining after a miscarriage. The hope was that the procedure would help me conceive in the future.

Two weeks later, I was admitted to Hinsdale Hospital for the D&C. It was going to take about twenty minutes, and they gave me sodium pentothal as a short-term anesthetic to produce a "twilight sleep." Afterwards, when they rolled me into the recovery room, I opened my eyes and saw a nurse wearing a very different style of nurse's hat. So with my words slurred and sounding like I was seriously drunk I asked her, "Are you from Saint Luke's?" I was referring to a hospital in Chicago where I had seen the same nurse's hats.

She turned around to face me and asked me to repeat myself. I did so, very slowly, still slurring the sentence mercilessly. "Are you from St. Luke's?" She caught it this time around but answered my question with a question.

"Are you a nurse? Is that why you recognized my hat?"

"NO! I'm an Epistolopian!" I shouted.

The nurse laughed.

"If you can say Epistolopian, you can go up to your room. You look like my Aunt Mary with your beautiful red hair. Now I know what she would look like if she had one too many drinks," she said. She opened the double door into the hallway and called out, "Make way for the Epistolopian!" She was still laughing as she pushed the gurney into my room.

Joe was standing by the door, waiting for me. I looked at his big smile and addressed him in my slurred voice.

"This is fun. I'm floating near the ceiling and I can see the bed near the floor. Floating is nice, I don't even feel like I have a body. Do you think that drug addicts feel like this?"

It took nearly three hours of periodic checks until the drug wore off. Joe just kept asking how high over the bed I was so he could tell how close I was to normal. When I finally "landed," my speech returned to normal and we had a lot to talk over.

The doctor came in and explained that everything had gone well, and he wanted me to stay overnight. He said he'd be in early the next morning and if everything was fine, I would be discharged about noon.

Joe called his boss to tell him my surgery went well, but he needed to take me home about noon the next day. Joe wanted to know if he should come in early and work until eleven-thirty that morning until he had to take me home. The boss said to take the day off. It was a good thing we got our car when we did. It made everything so much easier

I was discharged on Friday, October twenty-ninth. Three days later, it was our third wedding anniversary and I was ready to go out. Joe surprised me with a wrapped box and when I opened it, there was a small, black cross with three tiny pearls forming a shamrock outlined in gold, complete with a golden chain. I still treasure it. I went to a mirror to try it on and was filled with joy. I smiled and turned to Joe.

"It's beautiful and perfect with this dress," I said. Then I gave him a hug and a kiss.

"Edie darling, go back and stand in front of the mirror and shut your eyes. Just stand still for a minute and I'll be right back." I heard him walk away and return. "Are your eyes still shut?" I nodded yes. I felt him put something over my shoulders and he said, "Open your eyes." I was overwhelmed when I saw what he had given me. It was a fur stole. I didn't know what kind of fur it was, but it was beautiful and very stylish. I felt like a queen.

* * * * *

November sped by with Christmas shopping and preparing for Thanksgiving. We invited my father's sister, my favorite Aunt Grace, to spend Christmas with us, along with

Liz and Gordon for dinner. Liz was due to have her baby in about three or four weeks and was glad she didn't have to do the entertaining,

Aunt Grace arrived two days before Christmas. She still lived in Hyde Park, in the same house where my father stayed when he needed to be closer to work, back when I was a child. She had taught fifth grade for many years and some of her students were children of professors and often very bright. They enjoyed her teaching because she was very interesting and had a generous sense of humor.

Grace had us popping popcorn to string with cranberries to make a decoration for the tree. Joe strung the lights onto the evergreen boughs and placed an angel on the top. Later, we all bundled up and went to midnight mass at St. Andrew's.

On New Year's Eve, Liz gave birth to my first nephew, Barry Livingston Cobb. What a glorious year we had. Thanks be to God. Amen.

Chapter 18

Joy, Joy And More Joy

———

The year was 1956, and we were racing toward fulfillment of my dream and Joe's hope.

Eloise Brown, a fellow teacher I had met while teaching at Highland School, offered to give me a baby shower in July. I was in my eighth month. We invited many of my friends from my years at high school, junior college, and Northwestern and had a wonderful reunion.

Back in those days, there was no way to tell the sex of the baby to be, so I received two outfits for a newborn, which are still in my cedar chest, along with blankets, hand-knitted booties, sleeping clothes, and all sorts of practical things a baby needs. We shared stories, and advice from older mothers who were Mama's friends, and several young moms too.

When I arrived home, Joe was amazed at the number of gifts I had received.

"Does a baby need all that stuff? Or are your friends just over generous?" he asked.

"Yes, my dear, to both those questions," I replied, "but many of them are for a six-month-old baby so he or she will have something that fits later."

Our son, Stephen John, was born on Saturday, September first, at La Grange Memorial Hospital. I chose the hospital because it had "rooming in," which meant the baby could stay with me, so I could nurse him instead of bottle feed him. On my floor, there was a lovely nurse with a strong southern accent, and you could hear her talking and singing to the babies when she would take them from the nursery to their mothers.

"Now you hush you little cutie, y'all don't need to fuss, I'm taking you to your mama and she's gonna feed you," she would say.

She brought even more joy to the patients with her appreciation for the new lives! While Steve and I were getting acquainted at the hospital, Daddy Joe was obviously tired. My labor had started at ten at night, but I did not awaken him until four-thirty in the morning to drive me to the hospital. He had only slept for four hours, and I had not slept at all, so I wanted to sleep too. After he held his son for the first time, I suggested that he go home and take a nap. Joe was conflicted by my request. He obviously didn't want to leave. I started to explain that I had been in labor for eight hours, and then I just dropped off to sleep in the middle of my sentence! He got home about eleven-thirty. With great excitement, he told Mama she had another grandson. When she found out that Steve had been born at eight-thirty in the morning, she fussed at Joe for not calling sooner.

About four o'clock in the afternoon, Joe returned carrying a large bouquet of cut flowers and a wrapped package with a blue bow on it. It contained a lovely pale, pink bed jacket. It was elegant and covered my hospital gown with style. After we had filled a good bit of time with hugs, kisses, and cozy conversation, we decided to go look at our son through the nursery window. We were both so happy and thanked God for such a wonderful gift.

Joe had been a busy bee while I was at the hospital. Although he had come to visit me every night after work, he had put together the crib which my sister Lizzie and I had both used as a baby and now, three years later, it was Steve's turn to use it. So Steve's official bed was the one I had slept in, which had resided in the attic for many years. A friend donated a bassinet and Joe decorated it with things we received at the shower. He placed it in the living room so Steve could receive visitors on the first floor.

Dorothy from next door visited us every evening and asked to hold the baby. She would hold him for nearly a half hour if he didn't start fussing, which he wouldn't do unless he was hungry.

It was a delightful surprise when he was old enough to smile. When he was born, his eyes were dark blue, almost navy blue, and I anticipated that they would turn brown like his Daddy's gorgeous eyes. When he was nursing, he would suck as fast as he could…slurp, slurp, slurp…for a minute or so, and then he would pull away, turn his head back just enough to focus his big brown eyes on me, with a broad smile and his face all aglow. It always tickled me, because I felt the message was, "Thanks Mom, I was so hungry, and this is so good!" Then he would return to nursing to get his fill. It was such a fun and satisfying experience that we were bonded forever. Lucky me.

The christening was held on October 5,1956, at Grace Episcopal Church in Hinsdale, Illinois. His Godparents were the Rev. and Mrs. Max Tracy (a.k.a., my friend Jude), and The Rev. Wilson Reed Jr., from Canterbury Club. Father Stroup arranged a private baptism on a Saturday since the Godfathers were both clergy and needed to be in their own parish on Sunday. Liz loaned us the beautiful christening dress that I had given her for her son Barry, and Stephen looked very elegant in it.

We had a small party after we returned to the house, and we invited the neighbors. The guest of honor lay in his bassinet, sound asleep.

Being a mother was my calling. I felt fulfilled. Joe was also very joyful and loved being a father. We decided early in my pregnancy not to tell Joe's parents that we were expecting. His mother was inclined to worry about members of her family, she knew of my previous trouble, and we didn't want her to spend months worrying. Once again, she demonstrated her psychic ability when she called our home while I was in labor at the hospital. Mama answered the phone and Stella introduced herself and asked for Joe. Mama told her that Joe wasn't home and Stella, said, "Is Edith alright?" Mother said she gasped and told her I was at the hospital having a baby, and Joe was planning to call her and Stanley as soon as he knew the news. Mama reassured her that I was in excellent health and that I had a top doctor and was sure that everything would go as God wanted it. They chatted a little, and Mama said she hoped she did the right thing. Joe called his family and promised them pictures, and all thought it was a wonderful blessing.

Steve's first year was pleasant. He was healthy, cut his teeth without much fuss and was soon raring to walk. He pulled himself up to a standing position at seven months by grabbing the slats on the inside of the playpen and walked around, grabbing one slat after another. Of course, this tired him out, and after a short walk he would slide into a sitting position, rollover, and go to sleep. He loved books, and we read to him daily. The year passed rapidly, and soon we had a toddler.

* * * * *

As we moved into the next few years of parenthood, I came to think of the preschool years as the period of kids, cousins, dogs, and cats. Liz, Arden, and I had a new addition nearly every year and the cousin birthday roster looked like th is:

1954 Barry Cobb
1956 Steve Vosefski
1957 Bruce Cobb
1958 Greg Vosefski
1961 Carolyn Cobb

Arden had her son Bob in 1955 and Susan in 1957, plus Kathy and Henry later. We were together frequently, and the children got along with each other and enjoyed playing together.

On October 6, 1958, Gregory Richard was born to Joe and me. Joe and I welcomed him with love, blessings, and thanks to our heavenly creator. He was such an outstandingly good-looking baby that when I took him out in the buggy, strangers would slow down and comment what a pretty baby he was. However, if they really looked him over and spied his broad shoulders, they would look confused and ask if he was a boy. When Steve was with us, he usually had a bad habit of slowing down and standing still. On one occasion, a lady stopped to admire his baby brother and Steve looked up at the woman, waved at her and said, "Bye bye, lady." I didn't know that Steve even knew the word "lady," but she took the hint and I was left to explain how that was rude, and he needed to learn patience.

For Greg, however, speech became a major worry. By the time he hit his second birthday, he still had not spoken a sound. No Dada, Mama, nothing. If he wanted a drink, he would grab the hem of my dress and drag me in the direction he wanted to go. Then he would point at the sink and at a glass if one was out where he could see it. I'd fill a cup and hand it to him, and he'd give me a big smile and drink it. I began to wonder if he was deaf, so I took him to his pediatrician for a checkup.

Dr. S asked me two simple questions after he had examined his ears: does he know his name and does he respond to it when called? I answered yes to both questions.

"Then he's not deaf," Dr. S said. "His ears look normal, and some children just take their time becoming verbal. He will most likely begin speaking before his third birthday. If he doesn't, bring him back and we will have to do some other testing, but I think you will hear something soon. If you have some of those cardboard-like children's books with a page of animals and a word with a sound below it, try reading it to him, day after day. *This is the picture of a duck, the duck says quack, what does the duck say, Greg?* Repeat the sound if necessary. Do two or three sounds in a session. Next time review the pages you did and give lots of praise if he remembers, then add one or two more animals. Babies and toddlers love to make the animal sounds, and it gets them using the right muscles."

The doctor was right. One day, a couple months later, he grabbed my skirt and pointed me toward the kitchen. He stood in front of the sink and announced, "I wanna dink."

"Here's your cup," I replied with enthusiasm. "Can you say 'thank you'?"

"Tank ewe," Greg replied.

"Wonderful! We're on our way," I said out loud, happily to myself.

Mama was so relieved when he started speaking. Greg was very fond of her. The two of them spent time together nearly every day, but bad news was waiting around the corner.

Mama had a stroke.

One day, she was in bed because she had a headache and wanted to get off her feet, when Greg went in to see her. I don't know just what he saw, but he came running to get me, grabbed my skirt, and pointed me to Mama's room. She was shaking and trying to speak, but her words were slurred, and she had a hard time forming them. At that point in time, Downers Grove did not have a hospital or 911 to call. I dialed Dr. H's number and told the nurse what was happening, and she put the doctor on the phone. He called the ambulance to take Mama to Hinsdale Hospital and said he would admit her to a room and meet us there. Helen from across the street was outside when the siren started blaring and when she saw it was at Mama's house, she rushed over to find out what was happening.

"You go with her in the ambulance and I'll stay here with the kids until Joe gets home," she replied when I told her about Mama. "I can stay late so he can go to the hospital too." I gave her a big hug as the men were carrying my mother on a gurney into the ambulance. I spent the ride seated right next to her, holding her hand and praying out loud, hoping she could hear.

There was a nurse waiting at the door, directing the paramedics to the proper room, and she told me to go to registration to complete all the paperwork. As soon as I finished, I was directed to a waiting room, where I sat alone, wondering what was happening.

Another hour passed and Joe came in, looking very concerned. He took me in his arms and sat down beside me. He told me everything was under control at home and Dorothy and her husband, Bill, had both volunteered to put the kids to bed. Stevie told them he would help too.

Shortly after Joe arrived, Dr. H came to ask us if we would like to sit with Mama. She was awake, and he thought she would want us with her. Her speech had returned to normal, which he regarded as a very good sign.

When we entered Mama's room, she gave us a big smile and said she was glad we were with her. The doctor had told her to rest a lot and that she was expected to make a good recovery. Then she gave us some more bad news.

"I have bronchitis," she said, "but they think that I will probably go home in three days. I have antibiotic IVs here and pills to take home, so it won't be long. Glory be to GOD!"

Chapter 19

COURAGE AND TENACITY

Mama came home from the hospital with her boots on, but we thought she would need to retire them, at least for a little while. She was told to get a lot of rest and go for a walk every day, because after further examination, the doctors decided that she did not have a full stroke, but a TIA (a Transient Ischemic Attack or mini-stroke), which is less serious, but a warning that she needed to change her lifestyle. One of her changes was siding with her grandson on the subject of getting a cat. Soon after, Joe was off to the basement workshop where he created a three-story cat perch with a scratching post built into the bottom area. When it was finished, Steve and I went to the Hinsdale Humane Society Shelter to see if we could find our pet.

We played with and petted three kittens. Steve favored a gray and white one, but I told him that I thought he wouldn't be much fun. He was not purring and did not seem responsive, so I pointed out a beautiful kitten who had golden red fur, with a white fur bib under her chin and white socks on all four feet. She loved playing with Steve and purred loudly, kneading her paws when petted. Steve and I agreed she was the right one, and she was a great friend for the next nineteen years. Steve and Greg were preschool boys when we adopted Katherine, and they had finished with college when she left this earth.

In our home, Mama's favorite chair was an upholstered rocking chair with broad flat arms, and the boys would often climb up on her lap together, or one would sit on an arm of the chair. Soon there would be a pile-up as Katherine joined them. When the boys left, the cat stayed and was rocked and petted by Mama, an event appreciated by both feline and human.

Somehow, we also wound up adopting a dog. It was half beagle and Manchester terrier mix, but just a little bit larger than a typical beagle. Greg named the little rascal Blacky. Blacky was very energetic and impatient. We put him on a very long leash with enough slack to use the whole back yard, but he chewed the leash in two. Blacky then had a very good walk up the hill and a joyful run back down, gamboling like a lamb with small leaps in the air. The neighbors thought it was hilarious, but it was against the law. No dogs were allowed out of their yards without a human on the other end of a leash. So Joe bought some lumber, and built a fence that covered an area that was open from the back steps of the house to the garage. The fence enclosed the whole of the yard, since the other three sides were already covered with chain link fence. The wooden fence was the last effort to keep the dog inside the yard.

The finished product was very attractive. Joe used boards which were about six inches wide and made them form a lattice pattern that looked like a hashtag or number sign with a flat board across the top. He also made a gate with a curved top. The fence was a natural color, five and a half feet high, but the top of the gate was about five feet tall. Darned if that dog couldn't jump it!

So after the police stopped to tell us if we didn't stop him from running all over town they would be charging us a fine, we placed chicken wire at the top and bent it over. Then, when the dog tried to jump over, he would hit his head. He quickly learned to stop trying to escape.

* * * * *

One day, a gift of good fortune came our way. Joe's employer informed him that the plant was making some big changes and they were letting several engineers go, but they would give him a fine reference. This enabled him to pursue an opportunity with a retired military officer. The Major was looking for engineers, preferably veterans familiar with military procedure, and able to qualify for top secret work. Joe passed all the qualifications and was hired at a salary that doubled our income. Wow!

The work was funded by a government grant, and for

the next several years, I didn't know what he did at work. He was allowed to share with me that it was related to the Air Force. He was very happy with his new job and eager to go to work daily.

The day after Christmas, 1959, we received a phone call telling us that our dear Aunt Grace, my dad's older sister, was in the hospital and had choked to death on a chicken bone. It was quite a shock. As she had no children, she left instructions to be cremated, and her ashes buried at the foot of my father's grave in the Clarendon Hills Cemetery. However, our mourning was cut short because another aunt, my mother's older sister, Caroline, offered Mama a trip to Italy, with all expenses paid.

Caroline had moved to Downers Grove about the time Mama had her TIA. She went for walks with her and kept track of her recovery. Mama checked with the doctor and was approved for travel to Italy. The sisters decided to travel by ship so they would be rested by the time they arrived.

Aunt Caroline was an artist who had headed the art department of Oak Park – River Forest High School for many years. She had studied in Florence, Italy when she was young, and had a degree from the Chicago School of the Art Institute. My mother was seventy-three, and Caroline was ten years older. They paced themselves appropriately and had a wonderful time, surrounded by the Old Masters. They also spent two days in Rome, sightseeing. Then they caught a plane to London where they boarded a first-class flight to

New York, changed planes, and arrived in Chicago.

Mama called us from New York to tell us when they would land, and Joe and I drove to O'Hare and brought them home. Both Mama and Caroline were in good health when their adventure ended, in spite of their ages. For the next week or two we heard all about the trip and looked at the beautiful postcards and booklets they had brought home.

When 1962 rolled around, my sister Liz and her family moved from Waukegan to Libertyville, which was about an hour away from Downers Grove. They were having a new house built and when it was finished, they invited us to see it. They didn't have it all furnished or decorated, but they did have a feature that was uncommon in homes back then: a pool table, complete with a player. His name was Ajax, and he was their stark-white tomcat. Ajax would line the balls up at one end of the table and swat them, one at a time, towards the pockets, then race down the table to watch them disappear into the hole at the other end. He loved playing and would sometimes even wake up the family by playing in the middle of the night. It was really fun to watch, and laughter prevailed.

Time seems to pass rapidly once you have children. It seems as if one minute you have a new baby, and the next minute that baby is old enough to start school. Steve would enter kindergarten the week he turned five on September first. This led me to open up his baby book and relive some of the things I had noted. One particular notation came to my attention, which brought a smile to my lips and the memory of being amazed at the event.

I remembered a day when Steve was three years old but getting close to his next birthday. I was doing housework and dusting when I heard a peculiar sound. I stopped what I was doing so I could hear better. I heard it again. Steve was about five or six feet away, standing in front of a mirror that was covering a wall all the way down to the floor, and he was spitting at the mirror. Very quietly, I asked him what he was doing.

"We are spitting at ourselves," Steve replied.

He reared up to the stance of a hero and with his arms akimbo, placed his hands on his hips and proudly swaggered with pride. Then he looked at me as if he wasn't sure I got it and explained.

"There are two Stevies, the one in the mirror, and the one standing in front of it. The one in front wondered if they could spit at each other, and you can see it looked like it was happening."

"OK," I said. "Have fun but get a small towel from the bathroom and clean the mirror when you're done."

I was utterly amazed that a three-year-old had that much ability to create syntax and concluded he would do well in school. It brought a smile to my face.

However, sometimes life is not always full of smiles. Mama was staying a week at Liz's new home. Joe, the boys, and I drove her, on a Sunday, to Waukegan, as the Cobbs had not moved yet. I was thinking about my happy childhood memories with Steve when my sister called me in a state of panic. She told me that Mama was very sick and I should come get her, because she needed to see Dr. H.

"Are you sure that's a good idea?" I asked her. "If she is really very sick, perhaps it would be better to call for an ambulance and take her to a hospital near you. If I come, it will take an hour each way to get her back here."

"She says she doesn't need a hospital," replied Liz. "Just come."

"I need to have someone to watch the kids," I said, thinking out loud. "I'll call my neighbor, Mrs. Leverance, and then I'll come. Pray for light traffic so I can drive fast."

When I got to Liz's home, my mother looked very weak and we put a bed pillow and a light blanket on the back seat, loaded her into the car, and I took off. I occasionally exceeded the speed limit and hoped the state police would stop me and escort me to the doctor, like they had in the past. No such luck. I drove straight to Dr. H's office and was able to park in front of the door. Liz had called them to say we were on our way.

I held my mother so she would not fall making her way through the door, which was about five steps away. They took her temperature immediately and called an ambulance. She had a fever of one hundred and seven degrees and told me she needed to get to the hospital, right away.

I left my car parked and got into the ambulance and

rode with her to Edward Hospital in Naperville. Mama almost lost consciousness halfway there. When we arrived, they told me they were going to pack her in ice, and I should go register her. Fortunately, Liz had put Mama's purse in the car, so I had her insurance information available.

I called Liz and she said Gordon was home from work and he would bring her and the kids to our house too. Next, I called home, told Mrs. Leverance what was happening, and asked if she could watch Steve and Greg while Joe came to get me. She said not to worry, she would make hamburgers for the kids, and asked what they liked on them. Joe hurried to the grocery store and bought the things she needed for cooking, dropped them off, and drove to the hospital to take me home.

He did his best to comfort me, but I was having a guilt trip, blaming myself for not insisting that Liz take her to the hospital in Waukegan. That evening, the house was in a state of chaos. We had our kids and their cousins sleeping on the floor in the living room and Liz and Gordon on a sofa bed in our TV room. After breakfast, Liz and I went to the hospital and stayed most of the day, sitting there quietly with hope. Mama was in a coma for three days, as a result of acute cellulitis. She finally gained her ability to speak.

"I don't like this," she said. And a minute later, she was on her way to another world.

Chapter 20

CAN A SACRED GIFT BE A MIRACLE?

My wonderful mother, Esther Livingston King, was laid to rest on June 25, 1962 at Clarendon Hills Cemetery. We had held a wake at the Toon Funeral Home, with Reverend Cook from Mama's church, conducting the ceremony. Our sons had many questions about death. How do you explain death to a two-year-old and a four-year-old?

We decided that we would not have them attend the funeral, but Steve decided he wanted to say goodbye to his "Gama." We decided that we would let the boys attend the wake in private, alone with Joe and me, well before the funeral. Joe was surprisingly articulate, telling them about angels and how God sent one to escort Gama to heaven, which would be her wonderful, new home. They were familiar with the concept of a guardian angel from their bedtime prayers, and we knew there would be many more questions to come, but they seemed to handle the day of the funeral very well.

We invited several of Mama's friends, and Arden came

with us and helped serve an afternoon-style tea, in which we celebrated the life of Esther King. We shared stories of admiration and also included examples of things about her humor and passion for teaching. Several of my friends also joined us, and I was surprised at how many of Mrs. King's former students paid their respects.

We spent much of July processing Mama's legal requirements and giving her clothes to Goodwill. Legally, she left everything she owned to me and my sister, to be divided equally. Liz and I met one Saturday and divided up her possessions. Mama had two diamond rings. I picked the one I wanted, and Liz took the other. There were also silver serving dishes, and we divided those without any rancor between us.

Finally, we were left with the decision about staying or moving out of the house.

"If you would like to have a different house, or build a new one, now is the time to do it," Joe told me.

We spent a few days looking at what was on the market and came to the conclusion that we were happy where we were. We called the bank which had sponsored Mama's paid-off mortgage, and they required three estimates from different realtors to come and inspect the house. They said they would approve a new mortgage, providing that we borrowed an extra thousand dollars to repair some tuck pointing in a section of the brick foundation.

What a delightful outcome. Liz and Gordon now had

a large inheritance and Joe and I owned a home which was fifty-percent paid off, the day it became ours.

* * * * *

August was busy, as I was getting Steve ready for his first day of school and planning celebrations for his fifth and my thirty-second birthday. School would start just after Labor Day weekend. Steve turned five years old, two days before school started.

Greg and I walked Steve to school the first morning. It was straight through the block onto the next street. A volunteer mother with a handheld stop sign was conducting traffic at the corner and making sure the kids were obeying the rules. Steve was excited and skipped across the playground to be near the door. When he came home for lunch, he told us all about kindergarten, and how much fun it was. I was also treated to hearing all about it again when Dad came home from work.

Greg was four in October, and November first was our tenth anniversary. Joe and I drove to Milwaukee to have dinner at Karl Ratzsch's restaurant. It was just as fabulous as it had been ten years earlier. Somehow, the rest of the year sped by, and Steve entered first grade.

On the first day of school, the parents of the first grade class learned that the teacher who was to start the year had been injured in an accident and would not be able to start teaching until October 1. However, Mrs. Grant, an excellent substitute, would start the class and stay until the new teacher was available.

When the permanent teacher, Miss Smith arrived, she was young and starting her first year in the profession. Being a month off of the schedule seemed to make some things more difficult. Stephen seemed confused, and he was supposed to be learning to read, but he wasn't.

During Christmas break, Steve would bring me books and ask me to read to him, and Greg was always included. They often wanted me to read the same story over and over until they could repeat it aloud. My attempt to find out if Steve could read any word at all, even though he recited them, puzzled me. I decided to have a talk with the teacher after the break.

One day about the second week of January, Steve told me he didn't want to go to school anymore. I asked him why.

"Teacher says I'm dumb," he replied. I was completely shocked.

"Are you *sure* that's what she said?" I replied. "I don't think any teacher would say such a thing."

"Yes Mom, she said I was *dumb!*" Steve insisted.

"Well, she made a mistake, and you are really very smart, but apparently you have some sort of a problem with reading," I explained. "We are going to find somebody who knows why such a thing is happening. I'm going to have a talk with your teacher. But you are going to have to go to school because the law requires you to be there."

So I hugged him to me closely and held him for a minute before I told him to get his boots on or he'd be late.

"Steve, are you alright?" I asked him. "Will you be able to go by yourself, or do you need me to go with you? Are you afraid of school, or your teacher?"

"No Mom, I'm not afraid of her. I just don't like her."

He put his hat on, grabbed a cookie from the cookie jar, and rushed out the back door.

Greg had seen the cookie so he asked for one too, and I suggested that we watch *Captain Kangaroo*. I needed that show more than Greg did. I needed to be distracted from the intense anger that was building within me toward that teacher.

I spent the rest of the morning thinking about how to approach Miss Smith. Finally, I sat down and composed a note.

Dear Miss Smith,

I understand that my son Steve is having difficulty learning to read.

I am eager to discuss this problem with you so we can work on a plan to help him. I would like to visit the class during a reading session so that I can learn what method you are using and be able to implement it in tutoring Steve at home. I will visit tomorrow afternoon at two pm.

Thank you for your attention.

Sincerely,

Edith Vosefski

When Steve arrived home for lunch, he didn't have much to say but he took the note, with a smile, and delivered it to his teacher. Since she neither sent a response note nor telephoned, I had Mrs. Leverance babysit Greg while I went to the school. I timed it so I could observe the phonics lesson and have time to talk with her while the kids were out of the room at recess. Shortly after I started to talk, she put her arm on mine and stopped me. She looked me straight in the eye.

"Mrs. Vosefski," she said, "I think that you need to realize that Steve has limited capabilities and you should not expect too much of him."

Just then I wanted to scream at her, "You idiot! You think he's retarded?" But all I really said to her was, "I see!" And I picked up my coat and headed straight to the principal's office.

I told Mr. Langley, the principal, what I had just experienced and asked if it was possible to have the school psychologist test Steve's IQ. He first expressed sympathy for the result of my contact with Miss Smith and said he could understand why I wanted the test, but unfortunately the situation did not meet the qualifications for doing it. He said he wanted to help if he could, and he would explore various options, but to keep in touch in case I found any help. I felt a little better, but it was obvious it was going to be up to me to find an answer.

For the next two days, I was in a depressed fog. Ideas swirled around my mind, and I prayed for help. Suddenly, I found myself dialing Northwestern University and asking to be connected to the Dean of Education. I identified myself as a graduate of the School of Speech from 1953, and I told him my problem and asked if he could shed any light on the subject. He asked me many questions. In conclusion, he gave me the name and phone number of a doctor of psychology in the neurology department at the University of Chicago.

I called immediately, and the doctor became very interested in Steve's case. He told me that Steve's problem was new and fell into an emerging area of study called "dyslexia," which meant that the area of the brain that is used for word recognition was damaged in some way. Researchers were looking for ways to cure it. He said that he would be glad to do an IQ test and that he would be at a private school in Downers Grove on Saturday afternoon, where he was doing some testing. If I could bring Steve at three o'clock, he would add Steve to his day. Wow!

When we arrived at the school, the doctor saw Steve right away. They sat down and had a pleasant chat about the problem. Steve relaxed, and then took the test. The doctor told me that he would send the results to Mr. Langley.

However, the school would not pass on the result to the parents.

"But since this problem will probably take years to solve, I will tell you that your son has scored above the genius line," the doctor told me. "He doesn't need to know it. And don't use it against him, because the only thing we know so far about learning disabilities is that a person of good or high intelligence is unable to learn in a specific area that for similar people, would usually not be a problem."

* * * * *

The doctor was right. Years passed and when Steve was in sixth grade, I increased my prayers because he was going to attend Herrick Junior High, where they passed from room to room and had different teachers. At Washington, Mr. Langley had handpicked his teachers. Steve did very well with arithmetic and verbally, he kept up with much of the work because he was very good at listening. But in terms of reading, he was still several grades behind. Desperately, I thought, *there must be someone, somewhere in the world, who knows how to help!*

Chapter 21

SURPRISE, SURPRISE!

———

At that very moment, the phone rang. It was my sister, Liz.

"Edie, turn on your radio to your favorite Chicago station, right this minute," she said in a very excited voice. "We can't talk now; you don't want to miss a word of the program. Call me when the show is over." She hung up without another word.

My goodness, what a surprise I said to myself, but I did as I was told. The next voice I heard was Dr. K, a child psychologist from the University of Chicago. Dr. K. was introducing a guest, Mr. Jim Dhoran, who was a reading specialist in a public school. In the summer, he and his wife owned and operated a very successful camp that focused on reading. The camp was Camp Arrowhead, located in Minocqua in northern Wisconsin.

The camp had its own private lake, and the campers swam, played various sports and games, had campfires, etc. However, every camper was also required to put in an hour of reading every day. If a camper had already mastered reading, he could learn to speed read, or just read for enjoyment. The non-readers had access to reading specialists, occupational therapists, and staff members with a variety of related skills. By the end of the interview, I was sure we had found a solution for Steve, and I couldn't wait for Joe to come home from work.

After dinner and sharing the news with Joe, we called Mr. Dhoran. He invited us to bring Steve to his home on Saturday, where he would show us slides of the camp, and answer questions. He asked us questions and determined the depth of Steve's problem.

"Steve, you have a big problem, but I'm sure we can fix it if you can come for the whole summer," Mr. Dhoran said to Steve. "Have you ever been away from your parents for several weeks?"

"No," said Steve. Steve was then twelve years old and about to enter seventh grade.

"Do you think you would like to be at camp for that long, and that you wouldn't get homesick, and want to go home?"

"Mr. Dhoran, I would like to ask you a question. Do you really believe that if I stayed all summer, I would be able to read well enough to pass seventh grade?"

"Steve, if you are willing to do the work in the way we teach you, I know that you will be able to make the adjustment to a new school, and you will definitely be able to read."

"I hope you're right. I'll do it," Steve consented.

"Great. Now I want to talk with your parents."

"This sounds like a great opportunity for Steve," Joe said. "What is the tuition for the full summer?"

We both had our fingers crossed waiting for the answer. We had no cash set aside for summer. Today, the camp would cost around two thousand dollars. We offered a hundred-dollar payment to hold a place for Steve and promised to pay the rest when we brought him to camp. We had excellent credit and I was sure we could get a loan at the local bank.

On Monday morning, after the boys had left for school, I put on my best clothes to go to the bank. Just as I was ready to leave, the doorbell rang. It was our insurance agent who came to tell us that we had accumulated a large sum of money in dividends, and asked if we would like to invest it in more insurance. The answer was no, and we asked him for a check within a week, thank you. The amount of the check we received was the exact amount of money required, and it seemed like a good omen.

We were very excited and looking forward to the trip to Minocqua and seeing the beautiful Northwoods and lakes. As the drive would be about eight hours long, we decided we would stop at Wausau, check into a motel with a dining room for dinner and a swimming pool for Greg and Steve. It was a joyful place to be. The temperature was just right, and the sky was so free of clouds that at night the sky looked like it was covered with diamonds because the stars shone so brightly.

We rose early and set off for Minocqua, which was still two hours away. The road was lined mostly with pine and birch forests, along with warning signs to watch out for wild animals.

We arrived at the camp at ten-thirty on a sunny day. A person named Bob gave us a tour and arranged to have Steve's belongings sent to his cabin. By noon, we had paid the tuition and were sent to the dining room for a light lunch. We met various staff members who explained their jobs and any special equipment they used. A staff member came to us and said they were going to give Steve a Gates Reading test. Steve left us and we sat on a bench by the lake.

Steve returned to us, accompanied by an occupational therapist named John, who told us that Steve scored 2.1 on the Gates Test, which meant he had tested at the level of a second grader in his first month of class. Steve was very excited because he now knew his reading level exactly, and also knew how much progress he would be able to make at the camp.

The summer passed quickly for Steve and for us. We got a letter from him during the third week of camp, which was in his own handwriting. It was a short message about missing us and learning, but it was such an accomplishment for him to put those words together on paper. We were so thrilled for him. By the end of the eight weeks, he was tested again, and his Gates score was 7.1. Alleluia! He was at the beginning seventh grade level. After that, Steve became an avid reader and was like a sponge, sopping up all the books he couldn't read before.

The next summer he returned to camp for three weeks of reinforcement, and Greg went too, just for the fun of it. The third summer, Steve was a junior counselor and assistant to John, the occupational therapist. The fourth summer, they asked Steve to be a staff assistant again but received camp tuition and a stipend. He had found his career.

By the time he graduated from Downers Grove High School, he was a member of the National Honor Society. He contacted the University of Illinois School of Allied Health Sciences and was admitted to a five-year degree program to become an occupational therapist. After completing his degree, he passed his state board exams, and spent the next forty years working as a pediatric occupational therapist, specializing in treating children from birth to six years old with learning disabilities.

We are very proud of Steve. His intrepid attitude made him a winner. He never gave up.

* * * * *

When Greg was old enough to start school, we experienced one surprise after another. Greg was going to Washington School, where Steve had attended, and I had taught. It was 1962 and Mr. Langley was still the principal.

One day, about a week after Greg was registered, I got a phone call from a woman I didn't know. She had a thick, Appalachian, West Virginia accent and sounded like she could be a star on the Grand Ole Opry.

"Is this Edith Vosefski? Sorry, if I didn't get it right, but the office at Washington school gave me your name," she began.

"Yes, this is Edith speaking, what can I do for you?"

"Well, my name is Phyllis Mays, and I just moved here three weeks ago," the woman began in her slow drawl. "This town is very different from the one I left, and I have a son named Benjamin. I understand that you have a son, Greg, and he and Ben will be in kindergarten together. I asked Mr. Langley if the school had a lunch program. He said that the kindergarten kids had milk offered at recess time, and the mothers donated cookies or a snack, taking turns. Since I don't know any moms, I volunteered to be the telephone chairman, and wondered if you could help me with it."

"Yes, Phyllis, I'd be glad to help you. Is it alright to call you by your first name?"

"Oh sure, that's my name."

"Did Mr. Langley give you a list of names to work from?" I asked.

"Yes, but do we put them in alphabetical order and go down the list that way?" Phyllis asked.

"That's one way we could do it. Why don't we get

together and make a plan, so we don't miss anyone? Could you come over to my house tomorrow afternoon?" I offered.

"I'm sorry, but I can't. I have another son. He's Ben's twin and he is profoundly retarded and I can't leave him alone," she replied.

"Should I come to your house?" I asked.

We ended the conversation after she gave me the address. She only lived two blocks away. The next day, Steve wanted to play with his friend who lived two houses north of us, and I asked his friend's mother if that could be convenient because I needed to attend a meeting. I gave her Phyllis' phone number in case she needed me to come for him. Greg and I walked to the May's home, and he and Ben began a long friendship that day.

Phyllis and I worked out a plan which successfully enabled the kindergarten to have snacks with their milk. We also found that we had many common interests, which resulted in the growth of a close friendship. We both loved cats, and Phyllis had a beautiful Seal Point Siamese female cat named Toasty, which she had bred. Nine weeks later, they woke up one morning to find dead kittens, still in their sacks, strewn about the house in different rooms. Phyllis called me up to ask me if I knew anything about why a cat would act that way.

"Phyllis, I'm not sure," I began, "but my guess is she was in pain and didn't know what to do, so she began running around and when the kittens were falling out, she probably was so frightened, it must have seemed to her that she was falling apart. She must lack some hormone that keeps her from knowing she is giving birth. So be gentle with her and if she develops milk and becomes swollen, you better call a vet and find out what to do."

However, Toasty survived, and six months later, she managed to leave the house for two days and returned home pregnant again. Once again, my phone rang, and I was invited to start a new career as a cat obstetrician. So I jumped on my bike and dashed over to the cat. I had previously instructed Phyllis to get a good-size box and line it with a soft blanket, covered with a clean cloth to create a birthing place for Toasty. Phyllis had her in the box when I got there, but Toasty jumped out the minute I entered. I went after her and picked her up. She knew me and that I was trying to help.

"Now you just calm down," I told her, bringing her back to the box. "You are not going to run around; you are going to stay in this box, and Phyllis is going to hold you down."

"Oh, Edith, I don't think anybody has ever talked to her like that," said Phyllis, obviously surprised. I knew what had to be done from watching my own cats have kittens.

"Quick, hold her down and pet the top of her head and talk to her in a low, loving voice," I told Phyllis urgently. "A kitten is starting to come and she's starting to jump out. Don't let her go. Here's the kitten, but it can't breathe because it's still in the sack."

Quickly, I grabbed a nail file, slit the sack open, and removed the kitten. I laid the little being in the palm of my left hand and very gently began massaging his little tummy and chest for what I hoped was artificial respiration. About thirty seconds later, a tiny new sound came forth and he began to wiggle. The cat mom didn't have any reaction. I put the baby in the box with her and made sure that he found a tit and began to nurse. Somehow this must have turned on some hormone because soon another kitten arrived. Toasty bent over, chewed the sack off, and began licking the kitten. She delivered two more kittens normally, and I was delighted that animal instinct had done the job.

Chapter 22

ARTISTS IN RESIDENCE

———

My generous and loving Aunt Caroline was ninety years old, standing on the corner of Main and Curtiss St. in Downers Grove, waiting for the traffic light to change to green. When it did, she stepped off the curb and the car on Main turned into her path and struck her. Luckily, she was thrown far enough away from the car that it did not run over her when it stopped. The police arrived, called an ambulance, and told Caroline not to get up until the paramedics came. Once on the scene, the EMTs lifted her onto the stretcher and were about to place her in the ambulance when they heard Caroline's firm voice.

"I'm not going to any hospital," she said. "I am not hurt. I may be a little bruised, but Ben Gay will fix that, so put me down. You can walk me home. It is just the next building over, and my doctor has his office there. Oh, look he is coming out and sees me, I'll wave to him."

The EMTs managed to get her into the ambulance and motioned Dr. W into the cabin. The ambulance parked while

Dr. W had a quick look at her. He told Caroline that he wanted to examine her more thoroughly, and she should take the ambulance to Hinsdale Hospital.

"By the time you arrive, I'll be there," he said. In spite of her feisty attitude, he suspected she was in shock.

A couple of hours later, the doctor called me to let me know she had no serious injuries, but he wanted to check her liver and do some other tests too. He said that she was asleep and probably wouldn't wake until morning, so I called my cousin, Park Livingston, who was Caroline's nephew and her lawyer. Joe and I visited Caroline the next evening.

Several days later, it was decided that she was in no shape to return to her apartment and live alone. So Park helped her transfer to a nearby nursing home. We visited daily, and she told us how unhappy she was there, and how her landlady told her she could only go home if she had full-time help. Guess who offered her a home?

The vast network of Livingston nephews and cousins helped move her historically significant antique furniture (that had once belonged to some presidential family whose name I can't recall) into our home. Joe and I helped her decide which pieces she wanted in her room, and the rest went to various members of the family. We did our best to make her feel at home.

When she joined us, Greg was in eighth grade, and Steve was a sophomore. She got along with the boys quite well since she had been an art teacher for forty years at Oak

Park River Forest High School and was able to relate well to adolescents. Caroline told interesting tales about Ernest Hemingway, who was one of her students, and Frank Lloyd Wright who she disliked intensely. Mrs. Wright was a good friend of hers and when Frank took up with a mistress and dumped his wife and family, Caroline was disgusted by him. She never did reconcile his beautiful buildings with his "nasty" behavior.

Keeping Caroline happy wasn't always easy. If she misplaced something and couldn't find it, I was accused of stealing it. If women from her church came to visit, and I knew them and chatted with them as I walked with them to her room, Caroline told me I was wasting their time. If I merely gave them directions to the room, I was being impolite. About the fourth year she lived with us, she began throwing fits at the dinner table, which was our special time to connect as a family. She would get visibly upset, and begin to shake and cry, which Dr. W saw as a sign of dementia. It was upsetting to all of us, and it got to the point where I was close to collapsing.

"Enough!" said Joe in exasperation. "We are no longer taking responsibility for her. She can either go to a nursing home, or someone else in the family can take care of her, but this is the end for us."

I have to admit that I was relieved to have Joe take it out of our hands, and we called Park to let him know what was going on. He called the remaining cousins, but many had died. Finally, Caroline's niece, Marge, volunteered to take a turn looking after her. At the end of three weeks with Caroline in her home, she called Park and said she couldn't do it any longer. This made sense because Marge's husband was very handicapped following a stroke and caring for both of them was just too much.

I have to commend Park for what he did for her. He owned a very spacious home in La Grange. The north side of his house was an enclosed porch which ran the length of the house and was quite roomy. He had heating and cooling installed and added a bathroom with a shower designed for an elderly person, large enough for a wheelchair. There was a sink fitted with a chair, suitable for a hairdresser to come to the house to wash and style her hair. During the remodel, I made curtains to cover all the windows for privacy. I installed them so that sunshine could enter the room over the top or pushed aside for a view of the outside.

Caroline was well taken care of for the rest of her life. Dr. F, a doctor Park knew, made house calls periodically to check her health. She had been born in 1876, the year that America celebrated its centennial. There was a wonderful party for her one-hundredth birthday on the year of the country's bicentennial in 1976.She passed on the twenty-fourth of September,1977 at the age of one hundred and one!! May she rest in peace and may we remember her unique character, and the beauty of her art.

* * * * *

The surprises kept coming--some good, some bad--and others leading to life changes. One day during Aunt Caroline's stay with us, I turned on the TV to read a message aimed at women who had taken a drug many years ago that after years of further study had been linked to thyroid cancer. The message urged patients to call their doctor. This frightened me, because I had been gaining weight rapidly, without changing my diet. Also, for no apparent reason, I was becoming seriously depressed, though I was not unhappy about my life.

The message was repeated daily, and all the newspapers carried the warning too. So finally I called Dr. W He referred me to Rush Medical Hospital in Chicago to schedule an appointment with an endocrinologist, who was not only known in that field, but had a PhD in pharmacology too. She recommended a nuclear study of my thyroid. The test was negative, but Dr. G was very concerned with my weight gain and the risk of developing high blood pressure. She suggested another doctor in the building so I called her to see if I could get an appointment. By chance, Dr. S had a cancellation that hour and offered to see me if I would come right away.

Dr. S was charming, beautiful, and very smart. She was a board-certified neurologist and psychologist, and a true blessing in my life. Since my sons were growing up, going away to college, and getting jobs, she suggested it was time for me to figure out what I wanted to do with the rest of my life. She was so helpful that I saw her several times. She said she thought I had done a very good job handling Caroline and the family, and since I liked teaching and helping people, she was sure I could be a therapist or social worker. She suggested I return to school and get a master's degree.

I recalled that Arden had returned to college to complete her degree and qualify for a teaching credential, and Arden advised me to do it too. However, soon after, she and John decided to add to their family, and Arden gave birth to Henry. A year or two later, John lost his job at Argonne Labs, and the Schilbs moved to Aiken, South Carolina because John was hired to work on the Savanna River Project. We missed them terribly but managed to visit Aikin several times for our vacations.

I wasn't ready to return to school yet, but I began to study different careers and programs available at various schools. Joe and I discussed the possibilities. He thought I would be a good therapist, but he didn't like the social work program requirement of training in jails or prisons, so I crossed that off my list but kept an eye on possibilities for the future.

* * * * *

During the swinging sixties, we met a family who became very close to us. The Zweerts family arrived as refugees because of a horrible flood in the Netherlands.

Arnold Zweerts arrived in Chicago with his wife Julia, and ten-year-old son, Jan (who was in the fifth grade with Steve), a resume and a portfolio of artwork. He was hired at the Chicago Art Institute as a life drawing instructor. Arnold had been a young art teacher in England and Julia Brownfoot was his student. She was only seventeen, but Arnold was attracted to her from the time she entered his class, even though he was thirteen years older. She came from an art background herself, having a father who was a commercial artist, a brother, Andrew, who became a costume and set designer, and a mother who designed women's hats.

I've always had the luck to have many interesting people in my life. I was happy to meet the Zweerts because at that time, Phyllis and Bill had separated, and she and Benjamin had moved back to Virginia. Julia and Arnold became like family to us and because of that, I'd like to share a little bit of their fascinating story.

Arnold was a young man when the Nazis took Holland. He already had one of his paintings in a museum and knowing that the Third Reich was destroying or stealing art wherever they went, he traveled around and hid to avoid being arrested. However, after a year or two, the Nazis caught up with him and he was taken as a prisoner of war, transported to Dresden, and forced to work in a shoe factory and treated like a slave. He was there when the Americans fire-bombed the city. When the war ended, Dresden was overrun by the Russians, and he and the other prisoners were put into empty cattle cars to be shipped back to their homeland.

The Russian Army was so impoverished that they had no food for themselves or their prisoners. A guard with a rifle was placed in each car, and the engineer was instructed to stop the train if he saw cows or goats in the fields. The guards would leave the train and kill and butcher the meat. They had equipment on board to help make fires, and some of the meat was slightly warmed. Many of the men were so hungry they were willing to eat the meat raw.

At the end of the war, when Arnold arrived at the checkpoint where representatives were processing the different nationals to be sent home, he was put in the Russian line. After waiting for hours, he noticed the USA line was shorter, so he managed to sneak in. He was ultimately sent back to Holland where he belonged.

Years later, as our neighbor in Downers Grove, I always felt like Arnold thought I wasn't deep enough to understand his paintings. One day I spotted one of his new works and it made me shudder. The longer I looked at it, the more horror I felt. It was very abstract and the colors were dark black and indigo blue, swirling around the canvas with a tiny speck of ivory, which looked like a dirty white candle, and a fleck of yellow above it that looked like a flame about to extinguish. It was a very powerful image that I can still see in my mind, fifty years later.

The next time I saw Arnold, I told him the painting was disturbing and asked what he was thinking about when he painted it. He stared at me for a minute and let out a deep sigh.

"I had just finished reading the book about Treblinka, the extermination camp the Nazis had built in Poland," he said. "It ranked second in deaths next to Auschwitz."

After that conversation, Arnold and I had a new respect for each other, and Julia and I became friends for life.

Chapter 23

A VERY EXCITING TRIP

———

One summer day, after Liz had moved to Ocala, Florida, she was in town visiting and we decided to meet Julia Zweerts for lunch. Liz was delighted to make the acquaintance of a person from England. She frequently read English literature and the two of them had a literary discussion about their favorite English authors.

About two weeks later, Liz called me and said she wanted to go to England, but her husband didn't. She was wondering if I had any interest in going with her. I told her, yes, I was interested, and I would discuss it with Joe. I was very excited when I let her know I would be joining her.

"I don't have much money," she said, "so I won't be able to stay in big hotels or eat in famous restaurants, so why don't I plan the trip with bed and breakfast accommodations, and you won't have to worry about planning?"

"Great," I said, "however I also want to include a few days in Scotland."

Liz didn't like my suggestion, and we had a bit of a tiff over it, but I refused to go if Scotland was not included.

When I told Julia all about it, everything changed. She told us that her brother Andrew Brownfoot, and his wife, Margaret, were the owners of a four-hundred-year-old manor, named Stanshope Hall, in Staffordshire, near the Yorkshire border. It was located in a very picturesque setting, in a hilly area, with Wordsworth's River Dove across the road from the Hall. Both Andrew and Margaret were successful theatrical designers of scenery, room sets, and costumes in the English theater world, but to supplement their income, Andrew was a part-time instructor in an art school. They told Julia that they had decided to share their home as a bed and breakfast to personally recommended people. They were also available to drive people to places they wanted to see, at no extra cost. It was a deal!

Our flight into Heathrow was smooth, our luggage was loaded onto a bus, and in minutes we were in London. We registered in a small hotel on Curzon street, and I wondered if Father Curzon who married us, came from the same family. The hotel was next to Green Park, and two blocks ahead was Buckingham Palace. Liz and I spent three days wandering around London like typical tourists, but we solved the cheap food problem for lunch by stopping at local bakeries, which served hot Cornish pasties, warm Scotch eggs, or fish and chips. We added a can of something to drink and went to a park to eat, sitting on a comfortable bench.

The next stop was Cornwall and the town of Penzance.

The Town center had a large bandstand shaped like a gazebo and periodically played Gilbert & Sullivan music from the operetta, *The Pirates of Penzance*. The town was delightful, especially the little one-room booths which sold hand-churned guernsey ice cream cones, topped with clotted cream for an extra penny. Beautiful gardens and foot paths made walking a pleasure.

Next, we caught a train that took us North to Staffordshire, near the Yorkshire border. We were on our way to meet Andrew and Margaret. In addition to teaching, Andrew also wrote and published many books about different period styles which have been used all over the world by theater companies that produce Shakespearean plays.

As our train began to slow down for our stop at Derby, we happened to glance out the window and spot Andrew. He looked like a male version of his sister, so we were relieved he was so easy to find. He was standing on the platform looking for two women he had never seen before, so we walked right up to him and introduced ourselves. He was most cordial and saw to getting us and our luggage into his car.

On the way to Stanshope Hall, we discovered that the area was a series of low mountains with a rural atmosphere. It was sheep raising territory, and some of the roads were gated. Andrew would stop, leave the car, open the gate, move the car through, then close the gate, and walk back to the car.

As he was driving, Andrew told us that the first wing of

the manor was built in the 1500's. The estate had originally had many acres, but it was now being farmed by the farmer who lived in the Hall before them, who no longer wanted the responsibility of both the house and the property.

Over the centuries, the manor had expanded to have three wings. It was an impressive sight, but small compared to the magnificent homes of the English aristocrats. The interior was like nothing I had ever seen before. We entered through the back door. The kitchen was modernized and kept warm by the AGA cook stove and a pilot light that ran day and night. Off to one side was a door into the larder. The small room had the original stone floor and stone against a north wall with no insulation, so it would become so cold that the larder was used as a refrigerator. For heat, their cats would snuggle up to the stove since there was no central heating.

The next startling thing we discovered was a room they called the Lou Brary. Again, the room had a stone floor with a drain, stone walls, and heavy iron hooks embedded in the ceiling for hanging game or aging meat. Since this was no longer useful, they added a sink, toilet, storage cabinets, and many bookshelves. In the eighteenth century, the Hall added a drawing room and dining room, which showcased the talents of Andrew and Margaret with beautiful murals in the style of the time it was built.

Margaret was a gourmet cook. We had breakfast in the kitchen, dinner in the dining room, and coffee in the drawing room.

Andrew was our chauffeur and took us to see the many great estates in the area, such as Haddon Hall, Blenheim Palace (the birthplace of Winston Churchill), and the ruins of monasteries destroyed by Cromwell during the Tudor Reformation.

Eager as we were to go on to Scotland, we were reluctant to leave the Brownfoots. Nevertheless, we caught a train to meet up with our old friends, Phemie and Harry Brown.

We left the train at Motherwell, a town near Glasgow. Liz and I stood looking around and did not see them. We thought they were a little late and would show up in a minute or two. Then a woman we'd never seen before walked up to us and asked, "Are you the King sisters, daughters of Esther Livingston King?" We said yes, wondering what was going on. Then she introduced herself.

"My name is Dorothy, but call me Dot," she said. "I'm Phemie's sister. I regret to tell you that Phemie and Harry happen to be in Italy right now. When Phemie checked her calendar, she saw that she had failed to write the date of their vacation and had written the date of your arrival to be this day. However, in her mind she was thinking that you would arrive the week that they returned."

My anxiety was growing, and I wanted to say to Dot, "Get to the bottom line!" and then, she did. She told us that the house was empty and gave us the key.

"When you are ready to leave, lock the house and push

the key through the mail slot so it falls into the house," she told us. Then she pulled her car up to where we stood and took us to the house. She came in with us, brought out some cold drinks, and we sat down to get acquainted. Dot was very helpful. She gave us two different train schedules and explained if we wanted to go to Edinburgh, we would have to use another station to catch a train that went there. She stayed long enough to make dinner and told us we were welcome to use any of the food in the house and gave us the names of restaurants that were reasonably priced. After dinner, we went for a walk and looked over the town.

The next morning, we took the train to Glasgow, walked the two blocks to the other station, and went to Edinburgh. The skyline was dominated by the very large, royal castle perched on a high hill looking down on Kings Street and the Royal Mile. At least that is how it lives in my memory. I may be inaccurate; in which case you might just have to check it out yourself. Liz and I entered the castle and joined a guide who was escorting a group of tourists. It was very educational, and we learned many new things.

Then, as we were passing through a very long gallery with beautiful, stained glass windows, Liz and I spied the Livingston Coat of Arms and the name of Lord Alexander Livingston. I went over to the window to read the date and realized that all the windows in the gallery were a memorial to the men who had served over the centuries as the approved caretakers of the castle. It was a very powerful position, and Lord Alexander was most likely one of our ancestors.

We wore ourselves out in Edinburgh because there was so much to see, so we decided that the next day we'd go to the highlands, which would be more peaceful than the big city. We caught a bus that took us to a small town where there was a wool shop which sold tartan by the yard as well as already finished kilts. A very nice, older man was in charge and recognized us as Americans from our accents.

"And what are you two Americans doing off the beaten path?" he asked. I replied that we were visiting the land of our ancestors.

"Have you been here very long?"

"We spent last week in England. But you know, nice as England was, to my surprise, I find that I feel at home here."

"Well, don't you know that the English are a very strange race?" he joked.

I smiled and turned his attention to some dark green knee socks I wanted to buy for Steve. That spring, I had purchased four and a half yards of tartan from Pendleton, a wool shop in Oregon that manufactured tartan, and I had spent considerable time working on a kilt for him. The cloth was so wide I could cut it in two and sew it together to make the requisite nine yards needed for a properly made kilt. Julia had helped me get it right, with twenty-seven pleats across the back and every line matched. Steve deserved the proper socks to go with it.

We visited some of the glens and falls as we progressed north. We stayed in Inverness overnight and I treated us to a nice dinner and a lovely bed and breakfast. We noticed that there were many men in kilts and jackets walking to work carrying a briefcase. The road alongside the Ness River carried us to Loch Ness, but we didn't see the monster.

We arrived back at Phemie's house, cleaned it, and dropped the key and a thank you note through the mail slot. Then we headed to London and caught our flight home. It had been a real adventure, and we had coped successfully even without our friends. Whoopee!

Seventh Life

BACK TO WORK

Chapter 24

LIVES IN TRANSITION

———

For two years, I had been working five days a week at Calico Corners, a home décor boutique, selling and instructing customers how to use slightly flawed, high-end designer fabrics in their homes. Many of the customers were skilled sewers and were going to do their own sewing. I was responsible for figuring the yardage for their projects, but they had to supply the measurements of the piece of furniture or windows they wanted to cover. The store also had a workroom to do custom orders.

The job gave me two great benefits: my pay helped cover Steve and Greg's college tuition and as an employee, I was offered a generous discount. I was therefore able to make draperies and new curtains for my home, while Joe did an excellent job reupholstering some chairs.

The job had served its purpose and I was ready to start seeing the world. The trip to England with Liz came at just the right time because I had decided I was going to register for graduate school and start my master's degree in communication science with a major in interpersonal communication. That's a fancy name for learning how the words we use affect human behavior.

Governors State University had two campuses for this degree. The first semester was taught at a private psychiatric hospital in Des Plaines, Illinois. We attended seven straight hours of class time daily, with an hour off for lunch. We were allowed to eat in the doctors' lunchroom, and the food was excellent. We were being trained to work with borderline personality patients or patients with social problems who did not have advanced psychotic syndromes. We were trained with enough diagnostic skills to recognize when the problem needed to be turned over to the doctor. Our sessions were recorded, and the doctors would listen to some of them, and make suggestions, or praise us if we did a really good job.

We did not work with any patients who were admitted into the hospital. The class was made up of people who were seeking degrees to work in the mental health field. After we studied a particular form of mental illness, we students were assigned a case study and we role-played the therapist, the patient, other members of the family, etc. At the end of the session, the teachers would ask for feedback and give their own too. I found this type of experiential education to be powerful, exciting, challenging, and fun.

We had three weeks off for Christmas break and then we had to start an internship in a treatment facility. We required a place where we could serve three-hundred and twenty hours. I found a fully accredited alternative school, which was eager to have me, as they had previously accepted some students in the Governor's State program. They saw the teaching credentials on my resume and asked me if I would be willing to teach an English class as well as assist in the mental health field. I agreed, but I can tell you that Mr. Roberts didn't prepare me for these "students." Some of them had never studied anything except a huge vocabulary of totally unacceptable, dirty words. What a challenge!

The school was called The Pos, which was for "the positive." Although girls were allowed, boys between the ages of twelve and seventeen made up most of the student body. They were from broken homes and at least one of their parents was mentally ill or unable to manage their family without using violence against their child(ren). My students were therefore very hateful because they felt unloved and bewildered.

The principal at The Pos, named Kate, had a degree in social work and knew how to keep the kids' attention. We had a Doctor of Clinical Psychology on the staff, three teachers, and a psychiatrist who came to consult with us every Friday, to keep us inspired as we worked at our very exhausting jobs.

The school was located in an undeveloped area and was surrounded by acres of tall grass. At lunch time, the boys were allowed to go outside and eat their lunch, sitting on the ground. After eating, they could walk around, play catch, or explore the tall grass. One day they took a bucket out with them and found that the tall grass was a home for garter snakes. They entertained themselves by piling ten snakes in the bucket, then hurried back to the classroom where they emptied the snakes into the wastebasket next to my desk.

I saw the snakes, and with all of my self-restraint, showed no reaction. The room was quiet, so I knew they were just waiting for a scream out of me.

"Get your paper and pencil ready to write because today we are having a lesson about snakes," I said. "I have this encyclopedia volume that covers snakes, and I want you to write the name of the snake I am reading about, and then an action word in the sentence. I will write the name of the snake so you can spell it. Tom, can you tell the class what an action word is?"

As the grand finale to this exercise, I asked one of the boys to pick up my wastebasket, take it to the office, and show it to Kate. She would go outside with him and see that the snakes were put back into the tall grass. The boys were very disappointed they had not frightened me, but little did they know that my heart was beating wildly throughout the entire snake lesson!

When my internship was over, I was offered a job with pay, and stayed there for about six months. However, the next requirement for the degree was to take classes at the far south campus on Monday evenings from five to nine. That was two classes, back to back, and we were required to write a paper between forty and fifty pages on what we had learned in our internship, with examples of what we did. This was done on our own time and at the end of a month we had to report and defend our paper, in person, with the head of the mental health department. After that, completing the program simply involved putting in the class time and passing the tests. For me, the Monday night trips were a ninety-six-mile round trip. I graduated in August 1980, the week I turned fifty years old. We had a celebration, and Joe said, "Thank God, I've got my wife back!" The same year, Steve also finished his degree in occupational therapy and prepared for his state boards. Greg was studying history at Northern Illinois University.

Then, Joe came up with a good plan.

"Now that you are out of school and unemployed, this would be the perfect time to take a trip," he told me. "Here's an interesting ad in the Tribune. After you read it, tell me what you think."

After reading it, I told him the advertisement offered one of the best travel deals I'd ever seen. Northwest Airlines was about to launch a new plan to start traveling to Florida. The ad said if you bought a round-trip ticket to Florida and could prove you took the trip, they would sell you two, business class, round-trip tickets to London for the price of one.

We decided to travel to Ocala, Florida to visit Liz and her family. They had a lovely home with a large swimming pool, which we all enjoyed, and Gordon drove us to many historic sights. It was a very nice visit.

When we got to the airport, we asked for the connection to England. The representatives from the airline had never heard of the advertised deal. We asked the O'Hare staff and they also didn't have any information. I called the Downers Grove Public Library and asked if they had a copy of the Chicago Tribune on the date we had seen the ad. They did and I went to the library and made a copy of it.

Next, I called Julia and told her that as Joe had his ticket and I had my own, we were each eligible for the deal, so four people could go for the price of two. We offered her the use of the other two tickets. She told me that her daughter, Judy, was engaged to be married and was trying to figure out if she could afford to go to England so her aunt, Margaret Brownfoot, would design her wedding dress. They were to mail the pattern and directions to Julia, who would make the dress. This turned out to be the perfect opportunity, and we tried to get the tickets by talking to one of the airline representatives, but once again, they knew nothing of the deal.

Joe sat down and wrote a note to the president of Northwest Airlines. In the letter, he enclosed a copy of the advertisement. He wrote:

Since the employees of your airline don't seem to know what is going on,

I decided I was going to disregard them, and deal with the other end of the animal, who I trust will see to this matter. Thank you very much.

Three days later, our telephone rang, and a woman identified herself as the executive secretary to the president of Northwest Airlines. She said they had received the letter, and Mr. President had asked her to send us everything we needed to make the special arrangement happen. She gave us the extension for her private number and said if we had any trouble, to please call her, but she believed that all would go smoothly. And it did.

Julia and Judy agreed to go, and we set the date and were off to London. We flew through Minnesota where we changed planes to a larger, 747 model. We stood in line for several minutes to board. When we entered the plane, the stewardess, looking distressed, told us to stand still and she would be right back. She returned with her supervisor and explained that the business class section was already filled, and they would not be able to seat us except at the back of the plane.

Joe saw red and said that there was absolutely no way that would happen. He suggested that the supervisor call the president's secretary, as she had made special arrangements for us. I don't think she made the call, but within five minutes we were told that the first-class lounge was empty, and we would make the trip sitting there. Way to go!

There were four recliner seats in a row, each with a window. At night, they reclined almost far enough to be like a bed, and they offered blankets and pillows. We were on an upper deck, just behind the cockpit, and there was even a private bathroom. Gourmet food (of course!) was served on china plates with stainless steel silverware and crystal goblets for wine.

It was early morning when we landed. While we were waiting for our bags, Julia called Andrew for directions on which train to take and where he could pick us up. Soon we were off to enjoy the beauty of the English countryside.

On our way back to Andrew's manor, he said that instead of taking the major highway, he was going to take some of the backroads, where we could enjoy the scenery, and see some beautiful gardens surrounding several historical homes.

It was an excellent idea, and a real treat. We climbed a steep hill, came around a sharp corner and could see below us what looked like a possible sheepdog trial, which is a competition for sheepdogs and their masters to see how good they are at herding sheep. The car zoomed down the hill and Andrew pulled off the road into the grass so we could watch.

I was thrilled because I had been a long-time fan of watching sheepdog trials. I had even rescued a border collie from a farm where they were going to drown the pups because they were not purebred and could not be registered.

We watched the dogs work for about fifteen minutes and discovered that the farmer and his son were practicing because they would be competing in an official trial in the future. We wished them good luck and continued on our way.

When we arrived at Stanshope Hall, the design of the wedding dress was paramount. We also promised Andrew and Margaret that when they flew in for the wedding the next year, we would love to pick them up at O'Hare, host them in our home overnight, and drive them to the wedding in New Glarus, Wisconsin.

In the meantime, though, with my master's degree in hand, I set out in the world to find a new, exciting career.

Chapter 25

ON THE JOB

———

My new challenge was to find employment that would put my degree to work and pay well. I answered an ad from the Chicago Tribune for a social work position at a Chicago nonprofit social agency called Operation ABLE. The agency wanted to launch a job club for mature members of the workforce, which was a new idea that had been invented by an imminent psychologist and had grown over the years. Dr. A had written a manual on how organizations can start their own job club, and now, Operation ABLE was looking to hire me to implement his strategy and establish a club with them. The "ABLE" in Operation ABLE was an acronym which stood for ability based on long experience. The group was open to individuals fifty-five years or older.

The first group had ten men who were all dismissed executives. Some of them had been employed by the same company all their lives, and after twenty or thirty years, they arrived at work on a Monday morning to discover their computer was disconnected and their office had been packed into boxes. A security guard escorted them out the door.

At the job club, each man had a telephone for himself, and they were instructed how to make calls to potential employers. We had forms to use for the men to make their calls. If they weren't having any luck, they were supposed to tell us so we could help them improve their approach. If I listened to each man's story, I knew exactly how he should organize his information and present himself to a potential employer.

One day, one of the men passed out, fell to the floor, and I dialed 911 promptly. The paramedics took him to a nearby hospital, where he was admitted, and later we found out that he was short of money and had not eaten for three days. The hospital fed him, and one of the nurses gave him fifteen dollars. I helped him locate a relative who was willing to take him in temporarily until he found employment, which he eventually did.

Operation ABLE became so successful that the age to join was lowered to fifty, and the clients came marching in.

I had been there for four years when I received a phone call from the College of DuPage. The head of the adult basic education department said that my former supervisor, who had left ABLE the year before, had recommended me. She asked me if I would be interested in meeting with her for an interview and told me that the college had just received a grant from the State of Illinois to finance a program to transition people off of public aid by finding them employment. The program was particularly focused on those people whose youngest child was four years old, so they would be employed by the time the child was five. I went for the interview and was told that they didn't have any materials or books for the program, so it was basically up to me to create the curriculum. I told her I could do that, provided she could arrange a secretary to type some things for me, and make about fifty copies of each resource I would give the client. I said after that, I would probably be able to handle it myself, as long as someone else could do the typing.

My first day at COD, I had twelve students and gave them name tags with their first names in big letters. My first group was all women from DuPage County, mostly single mothers, who were very embarrassed to be on welfare. Most had come from blue-collar homes and had married young to less than desirable spouses. Some of them had a personal history of substance abuse. They were seated in chairs which were arranged in a circle, and I explained that the first thing we would do was go around the circle, introduce ourselves, and each answer a question in turn, speaking loudly enough that everyone could hear the answer. I looked at one of the name tags and decided I would start with a lady in her early twenties with sparkling blue eyes named Mary.

"Mary, I would like you to tell me at least one good thing about yourself," I said.

She sat there, silent and dumbfounded.

"Mary, I know this is hard, but there is something good about you," I encouraged.

"No! There isn't," she stuttered, after a long pause. "Okay, then I'll tell you what I see about you," I added kindly. "You have the most beautiful blue eyes. They light up your face and smile too."

"Thank you," she replied, showing off her very winning smile.

"Now, Jane, it's your turn," I said, turning to the next club member, a brown-haired lady, almost thirty years old. "Tell me at least one good thing about yourself."

"I can't think of anything," she replied, softly. "Then let me help you," I said. "How many children do you have?"

"I have three; ages seven, six, and four," said Jane.

"Well, you certainly have your hands full," I acknowledged. "Do you wash their clothes and send them to school with a good breakfast, their faces washed, their homework done, and their teeth brushed?"

"Of course," Jane answered.

"It seems to me that's a very good thing you do," I said.

On and on around the circle we went. Since the first two ladies had broken the ice, it was a little easier for the rest of them to come up with an answer, but it was obvious that on the whole, their self-esteem was in the sub-basement, when it needed to be on the second floor. When we finished the circle, we took a fifteen-minute break. I had baked some chocolate chip cookies and put the plate on the break table with paper cups and a thermos of cold water, because I knew people on welfare couldn't use food stamps for soda or bottled water.

Developing self-confidence was an important goal of our group, and by the last day, most of the women were able to recite five good things about themselves. We also practiced interviewing and knowing what to say, and, most importantly, what never to say. In most interviews, applicants field many standard questions and I made sure each student knew the answer that best applied to her. I was able to get the use of a television camera to tape everyone's practice interviews, and then play it back so that they could see what they were doing well, and what they could improve. The ladies generally recognized right away what they could do better and made strides to make it happen.

The group meetings lasted thirty hours in total, and on the last day, we called it graduation. I brought goodies, and to my surprise, the next thing I heard was everyone humming Pomp and Circumstance together. It was very touching.

Every other week, I had a new group of students and started all over with the new group, which was typically mothers on welfare. But sometime in the third year I was there, I once again had men in my class. There were three former U.S. marines who came home from Vietnam with serious Post Traumatic Stress Disorder (PTSD) who were having difficulty finding employment. They had all been through the Veteran's PTSD treatment programs, but about ten minutes into the first class, I learned an unforgettable lesson about how much they were still suffering.

My class was located in a different building, far from my supervisor. There was no telephone in the building I was in, so she sent a student helper to bring a notice to me about meeting with her after my class was finished.

Unfortunately, a marine I shall refer to as Bill, saw that the messenger was a Vietnamese young man, and instantly leapt out of his chair. Before anyone could stop him, he had both of his hands firmly around the boy's neck! The other two marines quickly pulled Bill off of the boy, who jumped up and ran out of the room as quickly as he could, even before we could check to see if he was O.K. Bill's buddies told me they had to drive Bill over to the VA hospital immediately. One of them ran to his car, while the other one embraced Bill in a tight hug so he couldn't move and patted him on the back continually, to comfort him.

"It's going to be okay," Bill's buddy said to him, trying to calm him as quickly as possible. "You will see your doctor and you'll be fine." Bill put his head on his buddy's chest, struggling to breathe, with tears streaming down his face.

Bill's other friend pulled his car right up to the door, and they drove Bill to the VA hospital, about fifteen miles away. I suggested that the people who were still in the class join me in a walk outside, and we could sit under an old tree on the grass if they would like to start the class outdoors. We needed a place where we could process what we had just witnessed, and hopefully develop an inner calm. After all, witnessing an attempted murder isn't a common life experience to most of us.

Later, I reported the incident to a security guard. They questioned me but the police were never called to get involved since Bill was already suffering from mental illness. He was back in my class when he got out of the hospital, and he was fine.

During my four years at COD, I was rewarded by helping so many people attain the skills they needed to get back on their feet. For example, once back in school, many of the people in my group feared the library. I introduced them to a resource that could truly help them move ahead in life.

A tall, thin, dark-haired woman we'll call Rachel was one of my favorite success stories. She had been abandoned by her husband with two teenaged daughters after being a homemaker for years. Since she could not pay rent, she ended up living in her car and spending her meager savings on a hotel room, one night a week, to do laundry in the bathtub and have a good night's rest. (Her girls regularly showered at their school.) One night she parked her car in a church parking lot and was approached by the minister there and given the help she was needed from a kindly lady in the parish who took her in and got her into our program. Rachel had once been a legal secretary, so with the help of our program, we got her into classes to restore her skills and she went on to a well-paying job with a higher salary than mine!

For a time, I ran into my former students on the job as waitresses and retail workers. It warmed my heart to know people were doing well. When I left COD, I was told that because of my work, 350 people had left the welfare system and I had saved the county about sixteen thousand dollars a month in social services. I truly consider this one of the crowning achievements in my life. I loved doing it.

Chapter 26

MY YEAR OFF

———

In 1984, I had to leave my position at the College of DuPage because the grant was cancelled so my job was no longer funded. My last day there was a time of true sorrow.

The night before, while we were having dinner, our clever border collie, Dogger, started making moaning sounds. I went and lay down on the floor next to her to hear her repeat the sound, and I could see her tremble. I put my head near her side, and I could hear the irregular, labored heart within.

While I stayed on the floor petting her gently and speaking softly to her, Joe called the vet and asked if he was still in the office and could see her. We wrapped her in a blanket and Joe carried Dogger to the car and put her on my lap for the drive there. When we arrived, the vet was there, holding the door open for us, and attended to her immediately.

I had already guessed what he would say. He told us she was having a serious heart attack. Of course, tears started streaming down my face. The vet asked how old she was and if we had gotten her as a puppy.

"Yes, we have had her for thirteen years," I told him.

"Then I know you took especially good care of her because the average lifespan for this breed is nine or ten years," said the vet. He was doing his best to console us. I gently bent over the exam table, petting her head and almost hugging her as she passed.

So, there I was with no job and no dog. I decided that I must be retired, and I was retired for two full weeks. Then I got a phone call from somebody I had worked with at the College of DuPage, telling me about a training job very close to my home that she had seen in the paper.

The company was looking for someone who was experienced in training and motivating adults. Now, that was a real challenge. The job was not for a low paying, nonprofit company, but for a very large corporation, the kind of operation where everybody thought the CEO was probably paid too much. I was most curious to see how I could fit into that sort of environment.

I called the number on the ad to apply to the job and was asked to come in to interview at a certain time. When I got there, the one trainer who was already employed was my guide to the interviewing room. The company was the owner of a natural gas pipeline that ran from Texas to Illinois, where the company was headquartered. There were two executives and the other trainer in the room to interview me. The chief interviewer seemed to be the overseer of the pipeline itself, and he explained the position well and then started asking some tough questions. I was vaguely aware that he didn't think a woman was right for the job.

He asked me a question which I no longer remember exactly, but it had something to do with motivating guys who were being promoted to supervisory positions. I wish I could tell you the exact question and the answer I supplied, but instead I remember asking for time to put my thoughts together.

They waited quietly, and then I remember giving a somewhat complex answer. Then all of a sudden, the overseer was interrupting me, almost shouting.

"THAT'S IT," he exclaimed, wildly. "WOW, THAT'S REALLY IT! MY GOD. WHY HAVE WE NEVER DONE IT THAT WAY?"

The other guy was shaking his head, agreeing. "Oh, lady, you sure got a head on your shoulders," he said.

I was excited, but surprised that the one who complimented me didn't know my name. I wanted to be sure he could recognize it on a paycheck.

I accepted the job, but I was afraid it might not last too long, because of a rumor about the company being purchased by the petroleum giant, Occidental Petroleum Company. If the rumors turned out to be true, I would be relieved. I wanted some time off in the summer to help Margaret and Andrew Brownfoot get to their niece's wedding in

Wisconsin, as I promised...However, if I really liked the job, I would probably only need to take two days off. Most of all, I wanted to keep my promises to both my friends and my new employer so everyone would be treated fairly.

February first was the day I started, and for a month I was learning things and doing some routine filing and office work. The next month was much more interesting and quite a different situation than the nonprofit job. They told me I was to be trained on the use of the Blessing -White Seminar curriculum in preparation for going to Houston to train the pipeline men who were being advanced to a middle-level supervisory position.

The seminar was to be held at the large Hilton Hotel on Michigan Avenue in Chicago. I was given a room for the night because the seminar lasted for two days. Breakfast and lunch were included. In the evenings, when we were no longer in session, it was like a mini-vacation. The other trainer, whose name was Paulette, flew with me to Houston, and we checked into a very nice hotel. Since this was her second trip to Houston, she acted as my tour guide and we went to see Nieman Marcus and to a crawdad restaurant for dinner. I had never even heard of such a food. I remember enjoying it but haven't seen one since.

The next morning the class began, and it turned out to be lots of fun. The guys were a bunch of jokers and asked silly questions, so we were frequently all laughing. They did pay attention to the things that they had to learn, but the source of the humor was their tales of adventure with wild animals along the pipeline. They shared their experiences so the new guys would know what to expect. They also kidded all the women with funny remarks about how we were all Yankees, but it was all part of the Texas culture and not disrespectful.

The rumors turned out to be true. The company was purchased by Occidental Petroleum in June and Armand Hammer, the CEO, said that the training department was to be replaced with their own people. So my luxurious job was over after only five months. Then, I decided that I should really retire.

Finally, I had time to improve myself. I was seriously overweight at that time, and had tried various weight loss clubs, I would lose a few pounds and gain it back, but if I didn't count every calorie, I stayed fat. I don't know why I had never asked for God's help with the problem, but I let Him know that I was ready to find the solution.

A few days later, on a Sunday morning, I sat down at our kitchen table and Joe had left the Sunday edition of the Chicago Tribune on the table. The sports section caught my eye with a story about a new quarterback for the Bears. I decided to read it, because I sometimes watched the games with my family, but I wasn't a real fan.

The article said that the new man weighed one hundred and ninety-six pounds. I felt like somebody hit me over my head. I was well over two hundred pounds and the very thought that I outweighed a Chicago Bear enraged me so much, I felt my prayer had been answered. I vowed right then and there that I would lose the weight without going on a diet or counting a calorie, but that I would gradually reduce the amount of food I ate, only weigh myself every two weeks, and not agonize over the results.

By the end of a year, I had lost seventy-five pounds. I still needed to shed about another twenty pounds, but I was able to go out and buy a nice, much smaller-sized dress, and a gorgeous hat to wear to the upcoming wedding.

The Brownfoot's plane arrived about four o'clock on a hot afternoon in July. It took about an hour to go through customs. We arrived at home a little after six o'clock and showed them to their room and bath. They wanted a cool drink and a chance to stretch after sitting for seven and a half hours.

When they were done freshening up, we took them to The Last Word restaurant for dinner. It had excellent food and was known for outstanding chicken and its Americana décor. Margaret told us that before they went back to England, she wanted to have a hot fudge sundae, and a malted milk. She said that she had seen them in American movies, and they always looked so good that she wanted to try it while she had the chance.

The next morning, Joe and I, Julia, and the Brownfoots started our three-hour drive to the wedding. The Zweerts home was in a very hilly area near the Swiss-style village of New Glarus, Wisconsin. This was an area of dairy farms and cheese factories. Beautiful flowers grew along the roads and fields, and Margaret, Julia, and I went out and picked a large variety of them to use in decorating for the wedding. We also stopped at a drug store along the way so Margaret could have her hot fudge sundae. She said she would go back another day for the malt.

The wedding was held in a nice building in a small local park. It was in a large room, with many chairs in rows, facing the front. A table was dressed as an altar, and the minister from the bride's church performed the ceremony. Her dress had turned out beautifully, and I complimented Margaret on his beautiful design. Margaret and I had worn hats to the wedding, and I think that I learned something new about hats that day.

I was sitting in the back row of the chairs, and behind my chair was a passageway to the restrooms, and a door to the building. My hat was made of dark blue straw with a raised crown surrounded by white chiffon pieces that were very striking and shaped like feathers. Many men passed behind me and surprised me by pausing to tell me how much they liked my hat. When the fourth man commented, I decided to keep count, and would you believe that seventeen was the total? Not one female said a word about it. I concluded that men like women to wear hats, and I have found the same reactions at church because I always dress for church. However, at church, the women tell me that some of them actually watch for me so they can see which hat I'm wearing. I find that both charming and funny.

Chapter 27

OUT TO SEE THE WORLD

——

Sometimes the nicest thing Joe and I could do for each other, in the middle of our busy work lives, was to plan another trip. At times, planning could be as much fun as the trip itself. We would pour over books, brochures, and ads, talk to a travel agent, and decide where we wanted to go. We managed to go to twenty-seven different countries in twenty-five years.

We traveled around the southern states where we had friends, and we called on Arden and John in South Carolina, Phyllis in Virginia, and my sister, who was now in Florida. These were very special trips because I never wanted to lose track of my really close friends, and I'm inclined not to write letters. We also included a few northerners: Kate, the social worker from the Pos, in Marinette Wisconsin, and the Zweerts Family in New Glarus. These same people also came to visit us in Downers Grove, so the friendships endured throughout our lifetime. If you noticed, I only named women; they all had husbands or a significant other, so Joe developed friendships with the men.

So much of the world is beautiful; the Canadian Rockies and our American Rocky Mountains are a feast for the eyes. I love the outdoors, the forests with wildlife, and the national parks. Nearby our house there was a wolf sanctuary, and I got to hold, and bottle feed a totally black, six-week-old baby wolf. Wolves are very interesting animals and they are my favorite animal to draw. I hope this little bit of a glimpse at what I just described will inspire you to travel as much as you can, and if you can't, your public library will furnish you with many free "trips." The librarians love to help people check out books, slide shows, and will even suggest music from a country you may be learning about. It's an excellent way to avoid boredom and see the world while staying home.

Now, I'm going to share with you the most unusual travel experience we ever had. The trip was sponsored by Northwestern University, and one of my classmates, Judith Richardson, also wanted to go with Joe and me. It was February, and we flew into Austria and stayed for six days in Salzburg. The historic old town was fascinating, and I was delighted with the beautiful way they decorated their buildings. They were often stucco-colored, and the people decorated their door frames with flowers, in garlands or pots on either side of the doors. It was quite a surprise to see such beauty in February! There was a shop that had eggshells of different sizes, all hand painted with scenes, prayers, and geometric patterns. Many of the eggs had a ribbon loop protruding from the shell to hang them as Christmas ornaments.

Salzburg was the birthplace of Mozart, and the apartment in which his family lived is still in existence. Music concerts were frequent, and the town could keep us busy all day. One day we went for a walk and when we were several blocks from our hotel, an American man and his son approached and asked us if we knew the location of the place which sold reservations for visiting the salt mines. We had just walked past it and thought nothing of it. We stood on the sidewalk, chatting with the man, and he told us what he knew about the salt tour. It sounded so interesting that we walked with them back to the ticket booth. We booked a tour for the next trip, which was leaving in two hours, and went to lunch.

We were escorted to the mine in a comfortable car. When we arrived, we entered a very modern building and were given some protective clothing to put on over our own. There was a jacket that had knitted cuffs and covered much of the torso. The pants looked like most sweatpants, with tight cuffs at the ankles. These outfits were necessary because we were to travel underground to the mine in a very different and fun way. There was a very large, highly-polished, wooden slide. It could hold several people, and you sat down at the top and went whizzing down to a distance two stories below. I loved it, just like a little kid. At the bottom of the slide was a large underground lake.

The guide herded us into a boat, and we rowed across the lake, where we found another slide that took us to the level where the salt was mined. About five centuries earlier, Celts had mined the salt, and now the mine was a museum. They had dioramas featuring miners working and a display of the tools of the time. Plaques with stories and information were everywhere on the walls. When we wanted to leave, they directed us to a modern escalator to return to the street level.

We entered the mine in Austria and exited in Germany. We were in a charming little village, surrounded by a beautiful lake and lovely mountains. At the end of the street was an old-fashioned ice cream store. Joe and I both bought an ice cream cone and sat on a bench outdoors, enjoying our cones while we admired the scenery.

We returned to Salzburg where we had a special dinner, and Joe chose an appetizer with red caviar which he said, "Makes me feel like I'm rich." That evening, we packed so we were ready to leave for three days in Vienna.

What a glorious city. We visited a famous chocolate house. The atmosphere made us feel like young lovers. There were young couples holding hands and exchanging quick kisses, so we did the same…why not? The ordering procedure was to sit at a table until a waitress came and found out what type of chocolate you wanted, and then she would direct you to a showcase where you could select from chocolate cakes, pastries, and petit fours, served on small, porcelain plates. At your table, your drink and a bowl of whipped cream were waiting. The same evening, we attended a dance program which was held outdoors, and people in splendid costumes performed Strauss waltzes. After they finished, the dance floor was open to the audience, and many people took advantage of it. The only real fault I ever found with Joseph was that he would never dance with me. His excuse was that he had two left feet!

At the hotel breakfast table there was a choice of coffee, tea, or hot chocolate with whipped cream, and a large assortment of many different foods. We had lunch at the famous Sacher Hotel and sampled their internationally famous torte. We took a tour of the opera house and a boat ride on the beautiful, blue Danube.

The Schönbrunn Palace was a magnificent place to visit. The first floor had forty rooms open to the public. They were decorated as they were when the royals lived there, and everything was exquisitely beautiful. However, the Austrian government had been very clever about taking advantage of the empty residence. At the time we were there, the rest of the palace was used to house retired people who had once served the country. I don't know if that is still the case, but it seemed to be a good idea at the time. The next day we flew home.

Another year, we felt we had seen enough of Europe and decided to have a look at the Pacific Ocean. We decided to visit Tahiti. We flew business class with Air Hawaii and the flight was comfortable, in a cabin decorated with Vanda orchids in abundance.

It was about ten-thirty at night, and dark, hot, and humid when we arrived in Papeete, the capital city of French Polynesia. We were transferred to a cruise ship, which was going to take us to some of the other islands and serve as our hotel. Papeete was a fascinating city which combined a modern city with many primitive crafts and features. A giant fish market sold the fresh, daily catch. Many of the fish were brightly-colored and resembled a larger version of fish you would see in a home aquarium. There was a Pearl Museum and jewelry shops which sold high-quality pearls.

We visited the pearl beds where the natives opened a small slit in the oyster and placed a glass ball inside so the creature would regard it as a foreign body and begin to cover it with the mother-of-pearl from its shell. It took months for the pearl to develop, and strict records were kept for every cultured pearl in progress. The longer the farmers left the pearl in the oyster, the bigger the pearl. At harvest time, the pearl was x-rayed and all of the information about the quality and thickness of the pearl's outer lacquer was given to the lucky owner of the pearl to prove its value in case they ever wanted to sell it.

We also visited one of the well-known islands in the French Polynesian chain known as Bora-Bora. It served as a naval base for allied troops during WW2 and the Corp of

Engineers built a very large airfield for bombers and fighter planes. The ship took us north to the island and transferred us to small boats to get to shore. As we left the boat, we saw a sign above a door of a primitive building which read, THE POLICE STATION. On the door was a piece of cardboard for a sign saying, *Sorry, had to go home for something. If there is an emergency, or someone needs the medic vac to transfer them to the hospital, call me immediately at my home number. And then he gave the digits, and the note continued. I will be back at one and the station will be open from two to four.* It was signed with the chief's name. They must have had a very low crime rate!

The movie star Marlon Brando had a home on the island, and many famous actors had their names listed on a sign in front of Bloody Mary's Restaurant. It was an outdoor restaurant with a roof over it, but no walls. The floor was covered with white sand which was raked and swirled into beautiful patterns. The food was outstanding, and the tropical drinks were fantastic.

We boarded a bus to return to the large ship. It was a flatbed truck with a box fastened on it which had been built on the island. Inside, it had seats and windows without glass on both sides. The bus driver spoke good English and wore nothing but shorts, not even shoes. He had decorated the bus with hydrangea flowers. We were halfway around the island when he stopped and parked by a coconut grove. He took several of the flowers off the walls and picked up what appeared to be a fishing line. He left the bus and motioned us to follow him into the grove.

The bus driver tied the flowers onto the fishing line and began dragging it across the ground. As he did, dozens of tiny land crabs came crawling out of the ground and began nibbling on the flowers, as Hibiscus flowers were their favorite food. When it was time to harvest the crabs, the driver explained that they were toxic and unfit to eat, so he would take them to his home and place them in an enclosure on the grass and feed them very small pieces of chopped coconuts. This would detoxify them and then when they grew big enough to eat, a crab dinner was served. As often happens with indigenous groups, many people seemed to see this tradition as primitive, but I marveled at the cleverness of some soul who figured out the whole process, and I wondered if he or she ever became a marine biologist.

Most of the people on the island were taught to speak three languages: Tahitian, French, and English. This made it very easy for the tourists, and easy to understand that this was a society of very gracious people. We said goodbye to the island, but it remained alive in our memory forever.

Chapter 28

THE SEARCH FOR A
NEW CAREER

———

I appreciated all the fine trips I took in my lifetime but decided that it was time to go back to work. I happened to be looking at a copy of the magazine, *Town and Country*, when I saw an ad for a training course to become an etiquette instructor and open a school or give private lessons. Having grown up in a very proper household where etiquette was important, I was immediately intrigued. I called the number in the ad and a woman with a charming, soft, southern voice from Georgia answered. Her name was Peggy Newfield and she owned The American School of Protocol. Peggy had constructed a clever group of lesson plans and a solid business model that made it fun to teach etiquette to children. I went to Atlanta for a five-day course and learned a lot about presentation for her. I was excited to be on my way!

I opened the Etiquette School of Northern Illinois in 2004, launched a website, and used our dining room as the school room. At first, I asked my friends to send their children and be my guinea pigs for the classes, which I held for one hour on a Sunday afternoon, for five weeks. We started with social skills and we taught the "magic" words: please, thank you, excuse me, etc. and we taught them how to shake hands without hurting any fingers. Then the instruction in table manners began. We served food and were very careful to find out if anyone had allergies or food restrictions. Joe acted as a waiter during the lessons and chimed in if someone needed a little help. We taught how and why you use a fork, a spoon, a soup spoon, a knife, and all the other odd pieces of silverware used in formal dining. By the end of the course, everybody could look at a table setting and know how many courses would be served that day. The children's favorite rule, which they found very funny was, "When you are at the table you should sit up straight. You bring your food up to your mouth, and you do not bend over and get your face near the plate. Only your dog or cat can put their face down into the food. Humans dine, animals eat."

On the last day, we asked everyone to wear their best clothes, and Joe and I met them at a private club which served superior cuisine and had a pianist playing quietly in the background. One of the boys announced in a socially acceptable volume, "This is the first time I have been in a restaurant that didn't have speakers!" He was most impressed. As it was graduation day, the meal ended with the presentation of finger bowls, in which a small flower was floating, and we all learned the proper way to use such a rare dish.

The school grew through word of mouth, as friends told other friends. I also networked and gave presentations at the library, the park district and to scout troops. The feedback from parents was always interesting. Apparently, the children shared what they had learned at home and had even begun correcting their mom and dad's manners in certain situations. Good manners are truly based on showing respect to everyone, while respecting the common traditions that many people already know.

Eventually, my unique class attracted media attention too. The school was even featured for seven whole minutes on the Chicago television station, Channel 7 morning news at seven-thirty in the morning. As you can imagine, my pupils and I had to be at the studio at five o'clock in the morning to be ready for the broadcast. The appearance led to other interviews too.

At some point I also thought it would be nice to have a book for kids which taught manners but did it within a fun storybook. So I invented a fictional little girl named Mariana, who was being ostracized from the other little girls in the neighborhood because of her bad manners. Once she learned new manners from her neighbor, Mrs. Proper, Mariana wrote her own book to teach others called Mariana's *Little Book of Manners for Children*. This was the first book I ever wrote but it wouldn't be my last! They are all available at www.EdithVosefski.com. I also wrote an advice column every week in one of our western suburban publications called "Hats off to Etiquette!" where I answered people's questions about manners.

The name of the newspaper column, *Hats Off to Etiquette,* was a reference to my favorite hat, the same one you see on the cover of this book. I used to tell my schoolchildren that the kind of hat a person wears tells people different things about you, and I'm from the generation that grew up with the starlets from the thirties and forties who always wore beautiful hats and white gloves. That became my uniform whenever I wanted to feel special. So one day I was at a silent auction that was raising money to move the Russian Orthodox Cathedral from Chicago to Des Plaines, Illinois. They had on display a collection of hats which once belonged to a Russian princess. As a regular connoisseur of hats, 1 knew immediately that it was a high-quality piece, worth at least two hundred or three hundred dollars, but I started the silent bidding at twenty-five dollars. At the end of the day, it was mine!

My etiquette lessons were helpful to people of all ages. On one occasion, I was asked to show a group of twelve and thirteen-year-olds how to eat spaghetti correctly. As they were being disruptive and not paying attention in class, Joe sidled over to one of the boys and said to him, "You know, if I was a thirteen-year-old girl, I'd want a boyfriend who ate spaghetti politely." It worked like a charm and they paid attention after that!

One day I also received an email from a thirty-year-old young woman named Rosa. She was Hispanic and had come to this country when she was three years old. She learned English in school, but her parents had expected her to marry after high school, so she never continued her education. She said that a doctor had hired her as his receptionist, and he taught her to do his books and keep the patient records in order.

At night she attended the College of DuPage for marketing, and was just about to graduate when she saw my ad. She asked if I might be able to help her with American do's and don'ts for the business world. I didn't know if I could help her but agreed to meet with her.

When she arrived at my home, she was wearing very high heels with faded jeans, and a tee shirt, looking rather sloppy. She had a nice face and lovely long black hair. It didn't take long to find out that she was very bright and would be able to handle a job with a bit of a makeover.

Joe was mowing the backyard when she arrived, and he didn't see her enter the house. When he walked into the room where Rosa and I were sitting, I introduced them, and then Joe excused himself and left us to the evaluation.

"You aren't going to work with that woman, are you?" he asked me, when Rosa was gone.

"I'm going to turn her into a Princess," I replied confidently.

The next Saturday, I met Rosa at a nearby department

store. I had told her to come dressed in something she would wear to work. I told her I would help her select attire that would be appropriate for her desirable employer. She told me there was a dental insurance company looking for a Spanish-speaking person who could speak to union workers. If she was going to be representing the dental insurance company to the union workers so they could buy their policies, I figured she would need something professional to meet with the executive, and then something more casual for meetings with the union representatives. I suggested she look at suits in dark colors--navy, gray, and black—but suggested a pant suit, with a matching skirt. She needed a simple, business-type blouse and perhaps a less-formal, colored top to wear with the pants. Rosa tried it all on, looked like a new woman, and she said, "Edith, I feel like Cinderella, and you are my fairy godmother."

I have watched Rosa grow into an account executive with a major health insurance company, find the man of her dreams, marry, and raise a bright little daughter, to whom I serve as a fairy grandmother. I love her whole family, and as I have no grandchildren, it has given me a chance to watch another generation grow.

All my life I have been curious and fascinated by people I have met. I enjoy getting to know someone and finding out how nice they are. I have been called naïve by people who think it's dangerous to talk to strangers, but I carefully choose those I converse with. If they don't respond, or are reluctant, I just shut up and figure the person is not going to have a conversation with me.

I have recently been reunited by email with two people who I treasure, following several years of no contact because they live half a world away. One day in late October, the phone rang, and it was Andrew Brownfoot, calling from England. He invited Joe and me to come and spend Christmas at his home. I was thrilled and told him I would let him know, after I checked the flights. When Joe came home from work, he was eager to go too. We had a month for our vacation time. and we decided to spend three weeks of it in London, seeing everything we had skipped on an earlier trip.

One of our first stops was the Crown Jewels in the Tower of London, and we agreed that they were magnificent, but definitely designed for a spectacular occasion. We went shopping to buy presents for the family, and to Fortnum & Mason to find something suitable for Margaret and Andrew. It was the first time we were separated from our sons at Christmas, and even though we missed them, we were able to look forward to our own family Christmas when we returned.

After our three weeks in London, we took the train north to Derby, and Andrew picked us up to take us to his home, Stanshope Hall. It was so good to see them again. We arrived on December twenty second, and Margaret had planned an open house type party. It was fascinating. I felt like I was seated in an Agatha Christie novel. A retired major and an older woman in a twin set sweater, a tweed skirt, and a style of shoes known as brogues, chatted together, and I half-expected the woman to introduce herself as Jane Maple. Apparently, a man of some importance had gotten into an argument with the village postmaster. The postal service was located in the only store in the village, and whatever it was that the postmaster said to him, the man was never to set foot in his store again. However, he added that he could not deny the man the use of her Majesty's Postal Service. Nobody seemed to know what they said to each other. Soon the topic of the postmaster's feud was exhausted, the conversation settled, and the mystery remained unsolved.

Christmas Eve service was at a very small, ancient church that was only used on special occasions and had no heat. It had a stone floor and some sort of a metal pipe that ran along the pews which could be turned on to create heat if you put coins into it. While we were singing carols and praying, a heavy rainstorm began, and we had to squish through the mud to get to our car. Apparently in Northern England in winter, there was snow on the ground as well as rain.

Andrew's home had central heating, but they only turned it on when it became extremely cold. They told us to tell them if we were too cold, but we managed. We had dinner at eight and between the main course and dessert, we all went upstairs to turn on the electric blankets so the bed would be warm by the time we needed it. All of the rooms downstairs had working fireplaces, and the first thing in the morning, the fireplace would be lit if they were going to use any particular room. The fire was built with cannel coal, which would burn for a long time, but you needed to dress warmly in the house to be comfortable.

We went out together for New Year's Eve and sang *Auld Lang Syne*. The next day, we headed back to London to catch our flight home, filled with wonderful memories from our friends.

Chapter 29

A DIFFERENT KIND OF TEACHING

I have never been good at doing nothing. Occasionally, I would entertain myself by going on a reading binge and read two or three books a week. In England, I picked up a documented book written by a man who interviewed the descendants of the notorious Bess of Hardwick. After reading another book, a historical novel about her, I was curious to learn more about Bess. When we were in England visiting the Brownfoots, we were in the county where Bess had lived. Andrew drove us around to visit Hardwick Hall and Chatsworth House. [KD1]

By the time we got home, I had decided to resurrect my acting skills and I wrote a one-woman show about Bess that I could perform. I auditioned for some women's clubs and was booked to present my show. My character was an imaginary cousin, dressed in Elizabethan costume, and I would make my grand entrance and explain that I was Bess's cousin. I told the audience that H. G. Wells had brought me to the twentieth century in his time machine. As her cousin, I was able to gossip about her and tell of her four marriages, how she ended her life as a duchess, and how she was considered the second wealthiest woman in England, next to the queen, her Majesty Elizabeth I. I also concluded the program with a short slide show of her homes.

This was a fun little interlude in my life, but I was looking for something steadier. I answered an ad in the local weekly paper asking for a certified teacher with experience working with children with emotional problems and/or learning disabilities. I knew instantly that I would like this job and would enjoy working with the faith-filled, very upright principal named Jane. I was hired instantly.

I was to be a "float" in the adolescent unit of Rockville Hospital. There were three other teachers who had yearly contracts, but I would be temporary. If there were enough patients discharged, I could be laid off.

Our students were transferred from their regular schools to the hospital school, which was fully accredited. The school would forward their books and lesson plans to our school, and the plan was demanding because we would have a small group of students in a class, each working on a different subject. In a fifty-minute period, I could rotate around the classroom. While kid one was working on history, kid two was studying general science, kid three was in an advanced college-level course, kid four was reading *Macbeth*, and kid five was analyzing *Huckleberry Finn*. Thank God for *CliffsNotes*!

I had to spend hours preparing for the diversity. I was paid for an extra hour of time for preparation each day. One of the teachers was responsible for teaching advanced math and sciences, so I was relieved of having to teach things I never studied. It was the students themselves that made everyday fascinating.

One of my students had multiple personalities. Jane had advised me that Ginny, a very pretty 16-year-old girl with long dark hair and a slender figure, often assumed the personality of a four-year-old named "Anna." I asked Jane how to handle it if "Anna" came to class. Jane advised me to have some art materials on hand which would be age appropriate for a four-year-old. I obtained kindergarten scissors, construction paper, Play-Doh, crayons, and chalk, just in case we needed them. On the first day, Ginny studied the conquering of the New World, and it went well. She was assigned five questions to answer for homework.

She told me that her multiple personalities, which she referred to as her "alters," had read the chapter and she wasn't sure she could handle it. I told her to do whatever she could, and if she didn't get it finished, we'd go over it together in class.

The next day, a fellow teacher walked "Anna" to my classroom because she said she was scared. Both of us assured her that she would be safe in my room. I told her that I had some wonderful art materials and that she could make a picture or a sculpture. I produced the materials, and her face lit up with delight as she chose the Play-Doh.

Then I asked her if she knew what history was, and she replied in a perfect, loud four-year-old voice that it was about countries and what they used to do. I asked her if she could think of anything about a country that she could make into a picture. She looked confused for a few seconds and said, "I can't, but Johnny can. He's eight and can make things."

"Alright, Anna, you go ahead while I talk to Marie, who needs to do some English. Is it alright if we tell Marie about who you are since she is going to be in the room with us?"

"I guess you better, but I'm not Anna, I'm Johnny, and I am going to make a flag," the sixteen-year-old girl suddenly announced, with the rather loud, bragging voice and swagger of a typical eight-year-old boy.

I turned to Marie at the next desk and asked if she knew what was going on. She said that she knew about multiple personality disorders. Marie then turned to Ginny and told her that she had a little sister who was five, and she was very comfortable with kids that age.

Marie and I had no sooner got into the English lesson than her psychiatrist knocked on the door and took her out of class for their private session. This left me alone in the room with Ginny. Or was it Anna. Maybe Johnny? Whoever Ginny was at the time was diligently working away at her art project and Anna explained that she was now Mona, who was five, and had come to help Anna because Anna was just too little to do much. But Anna had cut out a red paper heart for Edith, because she was such a nice teacher. In her best five-year-old manner, Mona showed me a very clever flag which she said Johnny had created from Play-Doh, "because he's older, and he can make things."

The educational goals and objectives of Ginny's treatment plan at this point were to make it possible for her to be able to enter a classroom and stay there for the entire period. We also hoped for some subject comprehension, but the former had to be realized before the latter could be achieved.   I wasn't quite sure what to do with a high-school level history text and a five-year-old student, but I had to give it a try. The experience turned into one of the most fascinating days in my teaching career.

"You know those questions you had for homework? Did you do any of them?" I asked the girl before me.

"My mother helped me write the answers because I don't know how to write yet," answered Mona with perfect five-year-old inflection. "And, and, and, I didn't know the answers to some of them."

"That's alright let's talk about the ones you do know," I said.

"The first one, I know what that word means, because we talked about it yesterday and I remembered. And you know what? Johnny doesn't even know that word, because he wasn't here yesterday, and so I listened good, didn't I?"

"Yes, you listened very well, and I'm pleased," I replied,

a bit relieved. So far so good. "The next word is 'viceroy.' Do you know what that means?"

"Oh, oh, oh I'm scared," Mona stammered. "Isn't that a gang of bad boys who could hurt me?"

"Yes, there is a gang of bad boys who call themselves that, but they live far away and can't possibly hurt you. But in history, the word means a person who is a ruler over a district or town, and the viceroy is appointed by the king."

"Does he wear a crown?" she asked, her eyes widening in interest.

"Yes, the king wears a crown some of the time," I replied. "Do you know what a district is? Because the viceroy is in charge of a district."

"What does 'appoint' mean? Like when you go to the doctor?"

"That's almost the same word. When you go to the doctor, you get an appointment. When the king appoints the viceroy, he asks him to take care of the district or town, like a governor."

Just then, Marie returned from her private session with her psychiatrist. She seemed very entertained with the situation. I asked her if she wanted to work on her English in the quiet room. She said she really needed help before she could go on, so she wanted to stay. At this point, I felt very uncertain about the best way to help either of my students, and I was also worried because I was certain Ginny's boisterousness could be heard in my colleague Pamela's classroom, who shared a wall with me. Eventually, we were once again interrupted with Ginny shouting and pointing.

"Who's that?" she yelled, once again looking frightened. She was pointing towards the front corner of the room and repeated, "Who's that?"

Maybe I'd been reading too much Shakespeare, but I almost expected to see a ghost as I turned my head to see what I knew was an empty space containing only a typewriter.

"That, th-th-that," she stammered, pointing to the typewriter.

I knew I had to diffuse the situation, but also help Marie at the same time.

"Marie, are you doing okay on your English right now?" I said.

Marie nodded her head yes.

"Can you go on without me?"

Again, Marie nodded yes.

I got up, walked to the typewriter and called Ginny over. I told her it was a machine, and it helped us to write. She settled down and cleaned up her Play-Doh. After that, she asked me to write her name: "Jake."

Later, Ginny asked if it was Friday. When I said yes, she became very angry and declared, "I hate Friday. Mona and me both hate Friday because Friday is the day you get wrapped."

"What happens on Friday?" I wasn't sure I had heard her correctly with her immature speech pattern.

"You get RAPED!!!" she said very loudly.

I was shocked, but had to remain calm, since I realized she may not have meant what she said. Still, I took the concern seriously.

"That can't happen here," I explained calmly. "This is a safe place, and we won't let anyone hurt you here. You don't have to worry about it; this is a very safe place to be."

The bell rang, she picked up her books, and by the time she reached the resource room, she no longer seemed to be Jake.

I reported all of this to Jane, who met with the student's doctor and passed on what all the teachers had reported. Ginny was in the hospital for well over a year. Her father was investigated by the FBI as a possible abuser, which upset Ginny because she loved him and insisted, he never hurt her. When he was arrested and about to stand trial, I prayed for her dad and the whole family.

Then, her doctor decided to use hypnosis, for a second time, to see if Ginny would reveal any information about her abuser, and after a few sessions, Ginny revealed the name of the man who had used her for pornographic photos, and eventually raped her when she was about ten. It was an elderly man known to the family who had frightened her with terrible threats if she ever told anybody what she experienced. He was brought to justice, and fortunately, she became an outpatient for several months while her doctor helped her adjust to a normal life. Alleluia!

When I left Rockville, Jane gave me a lovely review which I saved. Here is an excerpt.

Edith has joined the Learning Center staff with uncompromised commitment to her students, sensitivity to the educational demands of the Learning Center and devotion to the process of learning. Although Edith's tenure as a teacher in our setting has been a brief three months, her ability to "jump and land on two flat feet" has been admirable. Edith rolls with the pressures, questions the unthinkable and chuckles when she's faced with the impossible... Edith has shared herself with students and colleagues ...baking, personal collections, a sense of humor, hours of preparation, to attempt to satisfy course requirements for her charges...to create a school setting that promotes integrity and thoughtfulness.

Wow!

Eighth Life

WIDOWHOOD

Chapter 30

SURROUNDED BY GOLDEN LIGHT

―――

Most of my life I have lived in the sunshine of God's love. In a beautiful world filled with kindness and gardens, blessed with trees that blossom with fruit and plants that feed us all. At night, the sky reflects its silver light and stars shine like precious gems. Many ethereal clouds shed grace upon our land, supplying us with rivers, lakes, and sparkling waterfalls. An ancient Proverb reminds us however, that into every life some rain must fall, encouraging our growth as we travel life's road.

A storm that may begin as a gentle soft rain could escalate into a life-threatening storm. As old age approaches, life may become more difficult. As Benjamin Franklin once observed, "At twenty years of age, the will reigns; at thirty, wit; at forty, judgment." But I say if you make it to the age of eighty, you may feel triumphant and proud, and at ninety, aches and pains may dominate your life, but you do your best to feel better, even though perhaps you may start thinking about your relationship with your creator.

In 2015, the storms began. As Memorial Day weekend was about to begin, my dear husband was not feeling well, though he had seen the doctor early in the week. He told her he didn't feel well, but the doctor couldn't figure out what was wrong. She suggested he should see an endocrinologist because his blood sugar was rather high, and he also should get some extra rest.

The next day, he took to his bed and stayed there for three consecutive days. The third day, when I took his temperature, it was over one hundred degrees.

"Joseph, we either need to call the doctor, or get to the emergency room," I told him.

"Don't call the doctor. She doesn't know what's wrong!" he protested. "I don't want to go to the ER either."

"Okay sweetie, but would it be alright if I could find another doctor who specializes in older people, is accepting new patients, and has time to see you tomorrow?"

"Yeah, good luck." moaned Joe.

I went to our computer and searched for doctors. I found a page from the Loyola Stritch School of Medicine with very well-known geriatric doctors and found those listed in Downers Grove. I called the first one on the list and asked for an appointment for my very sick husband who did not want to go to the emergency room. She said I should speak to one of the clinical staff and transferred me to a nurse. She asked many questions and then suggested that we go to the ER. I told her he was refusing to do that, but he was willing to see the doctor. She told me to take his temperature again, and if it was climbing, to call the fire department and the paramedics, who would be able to convince him to go with them.

Then she returned me to the appointment scheduler. I asked what time they had available the next day, and she said that they had an open spot at one-thirty in the afternoon, but to call her again about one o'clock, because the doctor was so thorough with his patients that he sometimes ran late, as he always took as much time as he needed. I was further impressed and felt that I must have found the right one on the first try.

Greg's school was out for the day, and he came to our house and drove his father and me to the doctor's office. As soon as we entered, one of the nurses took a quick look at Joe and escorted him directly into an examining room. She fixed the table so he could lie on it immediately, and they didn't even know our name yet or if we even had insurance. Wow! She told me her name and said she would stay with Joe while I went to register him. I thanked her and she started taking Joe's vital signs and the information that nurses do prior to the doctor's arrival. While looking worried and anxious, Greg made himself as comfortable as possible in the waiting room, and I returned to be with Joe.

Shortly afterwards, Dr. S showed up, asked Joe several questions and began a very extensive examination. He commented a bit as he examined Joe, and I asked him a question if I didn't understand, and he asked me a few questions too. He rotated around the table and looked at or touched Joe from every angle. When he finished, he walked around to the side nearest me, bent over closely to Joe's ear and said, "Joseph, you are going to the hospital. You are much too sick to go home now."

"No, I'm not," said Joe, with all the spunk he could muster. "No, no hospital."

Dr. S took a big gulp and stood still for several seconds with a serious expression on his face. Once again, he bent close to Joe's ear.

"I'm going to ask you a very personal question, Joe," Dr. S began seriously and quietly. "Do you happen to have a good friend who is an undertaker? Because if you do, he will be the last person to say goodbye to you." There was dead silence in the room.

"You mean I'm really that sick?" Joe asked.

"The only way I can be sure what you are suffering from is by doing some tests that can't be done in the office," answered Dr. S. "Would you like me to call for an ambulance or would you rather have your family drive you there?"

"My family," Joe answered.

"Now Joe, you're not just saying that or going to change your mind?"

Joe breathed out a deep sigh.

"Yes, I'll go," he replied, relaxing into the pillow on the table.

The doctor then turned to me.

"Edith, I'm going in the hall to phone the hospital and when I return, I will explain the procedure and you can see it goes as planned."

He returned to the room with Greg, who had just arrived. Then he told us a person would meet us with a wheelchair at the door on the north end of the hospital parking lot. He would know our car from the description that Greg gave the doctor in the hallway. I could go with Joe to do the registration and paperwork while Greg parked the car. Joe would be taken to a private room to be seen by a doctor, and we could join him there later

"I'll be there within the hour," said Doctor S.

The hours that followed were filled with anxiety as we got Joe situated at the hospital and they assembled a team of specialists to see him. When we were told to return home and get some rest, I called Steve to tell him about his father and he said, "Shall I come now, or can I wait until morning?" We settled for morning, which was Memorial Day.

When we visited Joe, he seemed a little better, or at least more settled. Since this was to be a day of tests, we didn't stay too long, and promised to come back later in the day. We promised to bring him anything he wanted from home, such as slippers and a robe.

Time passed slowly, and then the doctors finally gave us the diagnosis. It was much worse than we had hoped. Stage four pancreatic cancer! We were devastated.

I called Deacon Tom at St. Andrew's Church and asked him about hospice care. Tom had spent many hours being active at a local hospice care, so he answered my questions. No decision could be made until Joe was able to come home. In the meantime, a hospital bed was delivered to our home, his pain was increasing, and the hospice nurse gave him some very effective pain medicine. Then he would sleep peacefully for several hours. When he was awake, he would talk with us and we'd plan the future and what he wanted for us after he was gone.

My last day with Joe was a privilege and a joy. A year later, I reflected upon it in a poem I wrote which described what happened, and my feelings about it. I called it, *New Anniversary.*

We celebrate anniversaries because life is good.
Weddings, birthdays, graduations
And life is good.
With so many auspicious occasions,
life is good.

Then one day
I pray the whole day asking God for a miracle
Because
I am on a death watch
but faith tells me that life is still good
My faith wavers and diminishes

And fear walks in the door
I am bereft of hope
I am losing my best friend
My lover, my husband of sixty-two years
I am split in half
So I call the hospice nurse, who tells me to cry
The nurse came and administered morphine
And he is out of pain
And that is good

My Joseph is semi-conscious for three days
The morning of the fourth day, he is wide awake
Smiling, wide awake when I entered the room,
Do you want breakfast now?
NO, KISS ME.
Love and passion arose to meet the request.
Life is certainly good.

What can I do for you now
Get me water
Water arrived with a bent straw and I held the cup to his mouth
Feeling an unseen presence in the room
Joseph looked up towards the ceiling,
His eyes grew big, staring at something
A smile covered his face.
Then his focus switched to me.
YOU ARE MY WATER ANGEL

God sent his angel to stay for the day
Joe passed peacefully a few days later
August 7 is a new anniversary
Because a divine being helped Joe to another dimension
His passing was blessed
And life is good indeed.

* * * * *

Two weeks later, a memorial service was held to celebrate Joseph's eighty-seven years on earth. We had programs printed to make it easier for those not familiar with the mass to follow along. On the cover of the program was a portrait of Joseph that I had drawn. We had a soloist sing one of my favorite hymns, On *Eagles Wings*, which was so moving, it brought tears to many eyes. Greg read the first lesson, and Steve gave a brief talk about his father, praising his dad's gift of love and patience.

Next, it was my turn to speak. I had written words to introduce Joseph's life, and his long-time devotion to his family. I decided that those who had never had the opportunity to experience his unique sense of humor needed to hear about it.

When Joe knew he didn't have much time left, he called Greg aside and secretly gave him a generous amount of cash. He instructed Greg to be sure he didn't let his mother know that he had this money, because she would want him to save it. Joe explained that the money was for Greg to invite his brother, sister-in-law, Robin, and his mother out for a very special birthday dinner because they all had a birthday in the same week. At the end of the meal, Greg should pick up the check, and announce "This is the first time in your life you have ever had your dinner paid for by a dead man!"

Laughter erupted throughout the entire church. A beautiful reception was held in the parish hall, and I was comforted by several people that I hadn't seen for a long time. A month later, Joe's ashes were buried in the columbarium in the church garden, with full military honors. And when my turn comes, I will be placed right beside him.

Ninth Life

RETIREMENT

Chapter 31

A LIFE WELL LIVED

Having arrived at the age of ninety, I've spent some time reflecting on life's meaning, and decided that it's a conundrum. A mystery, filled with opportunities, hardship, pleasure, and great love, fantastic people, and politicians nobody wants to listen to that spend their time arguing about who is right. But most of all, my life has been lived with an abundance of joy, and that took planning and foresight.

When you wake up in the morning, greet the day with a smile. Look out your window and if it's a bright sunny day, say thank you to the Creator. If it's raining, be grateful that you have rain boots and an umbrella. There is always something for which we can be grateful. Emptiness is spiritual bankruptcy. Surround yourself with people who are hardy, happy, and wholesome. Be compassionate when necessary for a friend, but don't dwell on people who have a negative outlook on life, unless it is for your career. The people to whom I dedicated this book are all doctors within different specialties. They not only cared for me physically, but they taught me how to care for myself, and for that I am grateful. There are also a few important people in my life who actually transformed my old age into a renaissance period of learning things I had never done before the age of seventy.

First and foremost is Jackie Camacho-Ruiz. Jackie was nineteen and I was in my seventies when we met at a Chamber of Commerce meeting and something magical happened. We became instant friends, in spite of our age difference, and discovered we were kindred souls. I was so inspired by her loving attitude, coupled with her "go get 'em" energy. When I was ready to start a business, I used her book on entrepreneurship for advice. I opened the etiquette school, and we did well enough, but I realized that I did not love running a business. I loved the teaching. Jackie encouraged me to stick my neck out and write my first book, *Marianna's Little Book of Manners.* Now, Jackie is the only publisher I work with, unless a larger publisher wants to promote my book, with Jackie's blessing.

Another new friend, Karen Forslin-Bojanski, was instrumental in helping my writing. She was the organizer for a networking group of authors. She was studying creative writing at the College of DuPage, and when a new class was about to start, she suggested that I join her and attend the class. She picked me up and drove me to the college, and on the way home, she invited me to join the writers group.

There were five or six people in the group, and most of them had also studied at COD. We critiqued each other's work and learned the do's and don'ts of good writing. In 2015, I began my second book, *"Leo's Out of This World Adventure,"* while I was in class. It is the story about the tooth fairy, who has a tooth museum in the Land of Lost Teeth, and it has a special tower where you can view the teeth of famous hockey players. Children find the story lots of fun. In 2017, I went on to write more about my protagonist, Leo. In *Leo and the Spirit Golden Boy*, Leo encounters the spirit of a horse with the help of a Native American farrier. We follow Leo to adulthood where he studies to be a veterinarian.

For my eighty-ninth birthday, Karen gave me an unforgettable birthday party. I had just had a terrible session in the hospital, where I was not expected to live when I was admitted. I was in isolation in intensive care for five days, and then moved to a regular room for seven more days. All medical personnel and visitors were required to put isolation gowns over their clothes and wear gloves before they could enter my space. I guess she may have thought that I might not make it to ninety, so eighty-nine was the big event.

Karen and I had a common interest; we had both taken up the cause of supporting Native American children. So when I wrote the invitations, I told my potential guests that I did not want gifts; I did not need another thing to dust. I asked them to instead make a contribution to any one of the Indian schools I supported, if they desired.

I collected the donations at the party with a box which Karen decorated, that looked like a school and had a slit in the top. I was treated like a queen and dressed the part. Karen had made me a necklace and earrings of beautiful, natural, yellow stones. My best present came when we opened the box of contributions and there was three hundred and seventy-five dollars in there! I added thirty myself and ended up sending one hundred thirty-five dollars each to the Navajo Nation in the southwest, the Crow & Northern Cheyenne in Montana, and St. Joseph's Indian School in South Dakota, where the children of the Lakota Sioux are educated.

Today I am an artist, but I had never dreamed of becoming an artist until one afternoon my phone rang and it was Olga. She had a Russian accent so thick that I could just barely understand her. She told me that she had just emigrated from Russia and was married to an American scientist. She had seen my name in the local newspaper as the chairman of the centennial anniversary of the Downers Grove Women's Club and wanted to know what it was and if she could join. She invited me to come to her house for tea so we could meet in person. I didn't know what to expect, but I was used to seeing pictures of two-hundred-pound Russian women who looked like stevedores, could lift anything, and drive an earthmoving machine. Oh, was I wrong. Those pictures were just propaganda to create a world image of strength, while we capitalists just sat around and painted our nails and bought fancy clothes.

When she opened the door, I beheld a very attractive, slender woman with blond hair and a lovely smile. She had been an early childhood educator at the rank of professor. She developed two training books for teaching both writing and learning numbers using art, in which the shape of the letter was a major part of the picture, and the children had to count how many times they could find the symbol. Then they could color the picture, so they also learned the names of colors. Her book was so successful it was distributed throughout the Moscow school system.

We agreed that I would help her learn English pronunciation, since she was already competent in reading English. In return, she would teach me how to draw. She was studying watercolor painting at the La Grange Art League school. She talked me into going there. They had the best teacher I ever met, and he turned me into a successful portrait artist. I think I was seventy-eight years old at that time. Don't ever believe that an old person can't learn new tricks. She can, if she is really determined, and still has her mind.

Add in a great teacher like Tony Crnkovich, and you can't go wrong. Develop a great friendship with a beautiful soul, and you might be moved to write poetry.

Olga
From silver
winter across the world

She
crossed the deep blue sea
Bringing
with her
The noble spirit
And
Fire of the dragon
To
Warm our hearts
With
Love

With heartfelt love, I want to say thank you Olga, for opening my eyes to the pleasure of drawing and art.

Some years ago, I attended a Pow Wow in Naperville, Illinois, where I met Joseph Standing Bear Schranz, an Ojibway elder. My friend, Karen Forslin, was with me, and she started talking to Joseph. They discussed the weather, and then talked about the thunderbirds, which Joseph said were winged spirits that protected us from harsh weather. I was amazed by what they said and when they finished their talk, Joseph turned to me and asked what I thought a thunderbird might be.

"Based on what I just heard, I think they may be some kind of special angel," I replied.

Joseph looked at me. "You catch on fast," he said. "If you are interested in learning about our culture, I invite you to visit our group. Call me and I'll tell you about the organization, and you can see if you would like to be a member. You do not need to have any Native American ancestors, even though our name is SOARRING, which stands for "Save Our Ancestors Remains and Resources Indigenous Group." I joined and am still a member.

There are two other Native Americans who are part of my life and both write amazing books. Quentin Young was a lecturer at the College of DuPage from 1998-2004. He taught a three-hour accredited course called "Native Americans and their Mystic Visions." He also lectured at several colleges and universities in Illinois with respect to Black Elk's vision and the Lakota spiritual way of life. The title of the book is *Mystic Visions: Black Elk's Great Vision Clarified.*

The second Native author I know only from his writing. He is the Right Reverend Steven Charleston, a retired Bishop of the Episcopal Church in the U.S. His meditations may be found on Facebook. They are powerful thoughts which make you think, and they are also breathtakingly beautiful. His first sentence in my favorite book, *The Four Vision Quests of Jesus* is, "My family has lived in America for thirty-thousand years." I think of the book right now, as the dreadful coronavirus is rampant in the land and the nation is in deep trouble.

Now in the midst of a pandemic, many people feel that God has forsaken them, and don't know what to do or how to vote. The riots and police, with their present methods for keeping order, are frightening. The politicians are either liars or trying desperately to help people who don't know the truth when they hear it. And climate change is causing forest fires.

Charleston's book is almost a road map for dealing with as much evil as is rampant in today's world, so I highly recommend you find it at your library or on Amazon (I receive no financial incentive for making this recommendation). I simply want to share a book from an author who I believe is wise, fascinating, and not as well-known as he should be!

In 2020, the big event I had been waiting for arrived! Cue the balloons and sound the trumpets--Ta da DUM, da DUM, da DUM! On August 27, 2020, Edith turned ninety! I made it. Wow.

I got up that morning, fixed my hair, dressed myself in my better clothes, used makeup for the first time in six months, and put a headband on my hair that some of my friends refer to as my tiara. About ten o'clock in the morning, my friends Terese and Mary Jane called and wanted to know if they could come over with their masks on and sing *Happy Birthday*. I gave them permission to do so, but asked them to sing on the patio, so I could social distance behind the screen door. It was fun. Some other friends showed up, and it was certainly a new way of visiting. However, the most precious moment of the day was when Rosa brought her little daughter, Isabella, to see me.

"You look just like a queen," she said, noticing my tiara.

"Today is Edith's birthday," said Rosa.

Isabella, who had just turned five, asked how old I was. I told her I was ninety, and she gleefully told me she was five and that she could count to one hundred. So she did. When she got to ninety, she said, "Happy Birthday" and continued on to one hundred. I loved it.

My sons gave me a lovely bouquet of fresh flowers, Jackie sent a very colorful flower arrangement, and Rosa brought an orchid plant. My sons ordered dinner from one of my favorite restaurants, and a good time was had by all.

EPILOGUE

———

In my ninetieth year, I am living in a country ravaged by a deadly virus and awaiting an election which I desperately hope will be able to change things in the country.

I am reminded of several quotes that summarize my feelings:

"All the great things are simple, and many can be expressed in a single word: freedom, justice, honor, duty, mercy, hope."
—Winston Churchill

In that quote, I think the prime minister summarized what our nation needs to learn. The "simple things" aren't so simple in a country filled with division; we can only get there with unity.

And also, Mahatma Gandhi's words pertain to us today...

"An eye for an eye only makes the whole world blind."

Right now, there is so much hate in the world. So many people believe an eye for an eye makes sense. Instead, all it does is turn people into warriors, just as it has in the riots we are now seeing across the country.

And finally, the words of one of our own great leaders, Dwight D. Eisenhower:

"I like to believe that people in the long run are going to do more to promote peace than our governments. Indeed, I think that people want peace so much that one of these days governments had better get out of the way and let them have it."

This is my fervent hope for the country, and the world moving forward from the year 2020.

Yes, our founding fathers made mistakes with their experiment in democracy and their toleration of slavery. It took several hundred years but we are now at a place where we agree that no person should own and mistreat another person, and from there should come the peace of the people he speaks about.

Also, my hope is that something good will come out of this terrible, unfortunate year that has had us all adjust to wearing masks, socially distancing, and protesting injustice. I have hope that if we do begin to realize and understand our unity, the future of our country will be what we want it to be and other nations may follow.

In other words, we must realize that love is the ultimate answer. It's the answer I have put my faith in for the past ninety years and I have no intention of stopping now. I hope my adventures in this book have inspired you to do the same.

Thanks be to God. Amen.

PHOTO ALBUM

College Capers

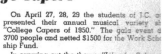

BOB DERRYBERRY
and
EDITH KING
Co-chairmen

On April 27, 28, 29 the students of J.C. a
presented their annual musical variety sh
"College Capers of 1950." The gala event d
3700 people and netted $1500 for the Work Sch
ship Fund.

In carrying out the theme, "Life of a Salesm
a troupe of Acne TV men were sent on a s
campaign to far-flung parts of the United St
One salesman became mixed up in a hot rod
pute, another fell in love with a farmer's daugh
The first act ended with harmonization by the
Foot Four" barbershop quartet and a portraye
a TV Studio in the confusion of rehearsal.

Act Two was opened by "Railroad Rhyth
the memorable choir scene, and "Mountain
tice," a salty sampling of the proceedings i
Tennessee court.

A salesman next infiltrated a UN lounge, a
to be ejected for downing too many toasts. A s
woman brought news of Acnevision to an Alas
base. After a tour through a living art gall
the results of the campaign were tallied and fo
to be quite discouraging. Faced with the baf
problem, Acnevision was forced to admit, "
is the end."

Dances included in Capers were a girls' tap l
a square dance, a Charleston, a boy-girl da
and a Can-Can.

(Left to right) Row 1—M. Hernandez, J. Brandt, C. Van Henkelum, E. King, R. Derryberry, Mr.
Stacy. Row 2—D. Oaldon, M. Deardorff, M. Rinehardt, D. Neas, M. Hoteldt. Row 3—L. Mills,
J. Haugen, B. Parry, J. Wilson, J. Dockum, E. Webber.

A GOOD MARRIAGE

IS LIKE A BEAUTIFUL FLOWER

WITH EACH NEW YEAR

IT WILL BLOOM AGAIN

Made in the USA
Monee, IL
03 January 2021

56263815R00174